FAMILY INVOLVEMENT IN TRANSITION PLANNING AND IMPLEMENTATION

PRO-ED Series on Transition

Edited by
J. Patton
G. Blalock
C. Dowdy
T. E. C. Smith

FAMILY INVOLVEMENT IN TRANSITION PLANNING AND IMPLEMENTATION

Michael L. Wehmeyer
Mary Morningstar
Doris Husted

8700 Shoal Creek Boulevard
Austin, Texas 78757-6897
800/847-3202   Fax 800/397-7633
Order online at http://www.proedinc.com

© 1999 by PRO-ED, Inc.
8700 Shoal Creek Boulevard
Austin, Texas 78757-6897
800/847-3202   Fax 800/397-7633
Order online at http://www.proedinc.com

Library of Congress Cataloging–in–Publication Data

Wehmeyer, Michael L.
    Family involvement in transition planning and program
  implementation / Michael L. Wehmeyer, Mary Morningstar, Doris
  Husted.
        p.   cm.—(PRO-ED series on transition)
    Includes bibliographical references (p.   ).
    ISBN 0-89079-812-5 (alk. paper)
    1. Handicapped youth—Services for—United States.   2. Handicapped
  students—Services for—United States.   3. Special education—Parent
  participation—United States.   4. Home and school—United States.
  5. School-to-work transition—United States.   I. Morningstar, Mary.
  II. Husted, Doris.   III. Title.   IV. Series.
HV1569.3.Y68W44   1999
362.7—dc21   98-49337
                                                                              CIP

This book is designed in New Century Schoolbook and Melior.

Printed in the United States of America

3   4   5   6   7   10   09   08   07   06

Contents

Preface to Series

The transition of students from school to adulthood roles has emerged as one of the most important topics in the field of special education and rehabilitation. The critical nature of planning for the transition needs of students has also been recognized in the school-to-work, often referred to as school-to-careers, initiative.

The PRO-ED Series on Transition evolved from a symposium convened in September 1994. Along with the opportunity for professionals interested in the practical aspects of the transition process to discuss many different issues, the symposium produced a series of papers that were published originally in the *Journal of Learning Disabilities* and subsequently in bound form as a book titled *Transition and Students with Learning Disabilities*. The current series represents an attempt to provide practical resources to transition personnel on a variety of topics that are critical to the process of preparing individuals for adulthood. Each book in the series contains valuable practical information on a specific transition topic. Titles in the series include:

- *Adult Agencies: Linkages for Adolescents in Transition*
- *Assessment for Transitions Planning*
- *Developing Transition Plans*
- *Family Involvement in Transition Planning and Implementation*
- *Follow-Up Studies: A Practitioner's Handbook*
- *Infusing Real-Life Topics into Existing Curricula: Recommended Procedures and Instructional Examples for the Elementary, Middle, and High School Levels*
- *Self-Determination Strategies*
- *Teaching Occupational Social Skills*
- *Transition from School to Young Adulthood: Basic Concepts and Recommended Practices*
- *Transition Issues Related to Students with Visual Disabilities*
- *Transition to Employment*
- *Using Community Transition Teams to Improve Transition Services*
- *Working with Students with Disabilities in Vocational–Technical Settings*

We hope that these resources will add to the growing body of materials designed to assist professionals involved in the transition process. The books in this series address the need for practical resources on transition that focus solely on specific topics.

Jim Patton, Ginger Blalock, Carol Dowdy, Tom Smith

CHAPTER 1

Overview and Introduction

The groundbreaking legislation that ensured access to a free and appropriate public education for children and adolescents with disabilities, Public Law 94-142 (Education for All Handicapped Children Act, 1975), also guaranteed family involvement in the educational planning and decision-making process. Cutler (1993), in describing the special education process to parents, summarized this act, now known as the Individuals with Disabilities Education Act (IDEA), as "a declaration of your child's educational rights and of your rights as a parent to *participate in the educational process*" (p. 3, italics added). Amendments to the act in later years funded transition services and mandated transition planning for students with disabilities, while redoubling the emphasis on family involvement (Education of the Handicapped Act Amendments, 1983; IDEA, 1990; IDEA Reauthorization, 1997).

The original act required that educators, in cooperation with families, develop an individualized education program (IEP) for each student with a disability. Amendments in 1990 (IDEA) mandated that the IEPs for students 16 and older contain transition-related goals and objectives. That age was lowered to 14 in a provision added in 1997 (IDEA Reauthorization). The act defined transition services as "a coordinated set of activities for a student, designed within an outcome-oriented process which promotes movement from school to post school activities" [§ 602(a)(19)]. Under postschool activities, the act included postsecondary education, vocational training, integrated and supported employment, continuing and adult education, adult services, independent living, or community participation. The act further specified that the "coordinated set of activities shall be based upon the individual student's needs, taking into account the student's preferences and interests, and shall include instruction, community experiences, the development of employment and other post-school adult living objectives, and when appropriate, acquisition of daily living skills and functional vocational evaluation" [§ 602(a)(19)].

This type of outcome-oriented transition process requires ongoing collaboration between professionals and the family. Professionals, including educators and adult service providers, advise the family about available options and the steps necessary to reach a particular outcome, and they are also responsible for preparing the IEP. But the student and family members contribute information, ideas, desires, and concerns to the process, and they always make the final decisions for the student's future.

Since the middle of this century, the level of family participation in education has been on the rise and is now approaching the ideal of an equal partnership between the family and professionals. But some barriers still remain (see Chapter 2). The purpose of this book is to present strategies that professionals can use to get past these barriers so they can foster successful family–professional collaborations.

1

HISTORY OF FAMILY INVOLVEMENT IN EDUCATION

Special education professionals today need to recognize that the role of the family in education has changed and will continue to change. For much of the first half of the twentieth century, schools were responsible only for academic instruction, while families were responsible for emotional and social development and instruction (Flaxman and Inger, 1991). Social upheavals of the 1960s and 1970s and changes in the structure of the family and society, including demographics, have significantly altered the role of schools in society and the role of parents in education (Flaxman & Inger, 1991). The contemporary notion of parental involvement dates back to the early 1960s when the passage of federal legislation designed to address societal problems mandated parental involvement in planning and decision making about curriculum, instruction, and school improvement. The Head Start program was among the first to employ such a model, bringing educators and parents of young children together to address both child- and family-related issues (Flaxman & Inger, 1991). Similarly, the Education for All Handicapped Children Act of 1975 mandated such collaboration.

Today, a new paradigm for human services, including special education, is emerging. It "envisions a social order wherein most important decisions are made at the local level. . . . and people are empowered to develop their own solutions to issues affecting their lives" (McFadden and Burke, 1991, p. iii). Recurring themes associated with this paradigm are empowerment, leadership, choice, and flexibility, and these now commonly appear in school reform proposals. Guided by this paradigm, professionals try to empower families by increasing their participation in the decision-making process. McFadden and Burke stated: "It is our belief that decisions that affect the quality of life experienced by people with developmental disabilities and their families are best made in consultation with and participation by the consumers themselves [people with disabilities and their families]" (p. iv).

Another reason for the increased involvement of students with disabilities and their families in decision making is the overall change in society's attitude toward people with disabilities. The new paradigm recognizes people with disabilities as *people* first. They are people with hopes, dreams, abilities, and interests, just like those of other people. They are neighbors, colleagues, family members, and friends—again like other people. They are also dancers, political leaders, baseball fans, stamp collectors, and dog owners. Most important, like other people, they have the right to live self-determined lives. In fact, the Rehabilitation Act Reauthorization (1992) and the 1993 amendments to the Developmental Disabilities Act both state that "disability is a natural part of human experience and in no way diminishes the rights of individuals to live independently, enjoy self-determination, make choices, contribute to society, pursue meaningful careers and enjoy full inclusion and integration in the economic, political, social, cultural and educational mainstream of American society" [§ 2(a)(3)(A-F)]. Disability therefore is not an aberrant condition but a part of the continuum of human characteristics.

POTENTIAL BENEFITS OF FAMILY INVOLVEMENT

Research studies have identified a number of benefits resulting from family involvement in the education of students with disabilities. According to this research, the benefits are greatest if the involvement is prolonged and if it begins when the student is still young (Sinclair & Christenson, 1992). Involvement leads to better school attendance, reduced dropout rates, higher educational assessment scores, and improvements in student attitudes such as self-esteem and confidence (Flaxman & Inger, 1991). It also bridges the separation between home and school (Sinclair & Christenson, 1992). Moreover, family involvement and advocacy result in better educational programs in schools and better resources in the community for students with disabilities (Sinclair & Christenson, 1992).

Families are essential in the development of the IEP, especially the portion devoted to transition planning. The other participants at an IEP or transition planning meeting—teachers, administrators, related service personnel, adult service providers—are likely to change from year to year and school to school. But the family members stay the same, and they help maintain continuity by providing information about students' previous transition experiences and services.

Families in general are a repository of information about the student: her strengths and abilities, likes and dislikes, limitations and idiosyncrasies. They can tell you how a student spends her spare time, what hobbies and interests she has, whether she has ever kept a checkbook, or has access to a computer at home. The student's sister can tell you how many friends she has in her neighborhood. Parents can tell you if their son can cook a simple meal, has ever interviewed for a job, or reads the paper daily.

Moreover, parents bring to the process their concerns or problems with the transition. Turnbull and Turnbull (1997) identified a number of problems encountered by parents during life cycle transitions, including the passage from secondary education to adulthood:

- Adjusting emotionally to the possible chronicity of their child's disabling condition;
- Identifying issues associated with their child's emerging sexuality;
- Addressing possible peer isolation and rejection at a time in development when peers play an increasingly important role;
- Planning for career and vocational options;
- Arranging for leisure time activities;
- Dealing with the physical and emotional changes associated with puberty;
- Planning for postsecondary education;
- Planning for the possible need for guardianship;
- Addressing the need for impending living and work environments.

Halvorsen, Doering, Farron-Davis, Usilton, and Sailor (1989) also identified transition-related concerns shared by most parents and family members: the discontinuation of support services that had been available through the school; the lack of appropriate adult services; the difficulty of acquiring information on available resources once the student leaves the special education system; and the need to plan for care after parents' death.

A final reason why families must be equal partners in decision making—they have the most to gain or lose from the transition process. When their child completes school but then either remains unemployed or has a job that does not provide sufficient wages to support independent living, it is the family that typically supplies a home and financial support, or both. One study found that, of 908 youth with learning disabilities out of school one year, 64% lived with their families (Sitlington, Frank, and Cooper, 1989). Sitlington, Frank and Carson (1991) found that three years out of high school 46% of youth with mental retardation lived with family members, while 31% relied primarily on parents for financial assistance and support. Moreover, several studies examining adult outcomes for youth with disabilities confirm that families become, in essence, the students' case managers. Sitlington and colleagues (1989) found that of 648 graduates with learning disabilities out of school one year who were employed, 43% found their jobs themselves and 40% identified families as having found their jobs for them. Only 5% found jobs through a community agency and 6% through school.

THE CURRENT REALITY: PARTICIPATION LESS THAN DESIRED

Although the involvement of families in the educational planning and decision-making process, and particularly in the transition process, is essential to adult success, in too many cases the parents and other family members are not active partners. In a study by McNair and Rusch (1991), parents reported being less involved in transition programming than they wished, and most said they wanted to take an equal part in the decision making but didn't have the opportunity. McNair and Rusch noted that parents also wanted more opportunities to be involved in finding job placements and community-living arrangements. They also found that the parents who were involved in transition programming were more likely to have formulated a postschool plan for their son or daughter. The lack of parental knowledge about transition programming and the consequent frustration with the process have been identified by others as well (Gallivan-Felon, 1994; Turnbull & Turnbull, 1997).

During transition planning, parents encounter a new set of professionals such as adult service providers and vocational rehabilitation counselors. The "insider" knowledge they had acquired about how to work the educational system does not transfer directly to this new situation, and parents feel as if they have to start again. Another surprise that may await them is the lack of "entitlement" programs that guarantee work or independent living for graduates with disabilities. For these and other reasons, such as those highlighted by Turnbull and Turnbull (1997), the transition period may be more stressful and anxiety provoking, not to mention confusing, than when the adolescent was a young child.

Educators can do much to ease these concerns and facilitate effective parental and family involvement in transition. They can explain the concept of transition and transition services to parents, make them aware of mandates in the law, and provide them with the knowledge needed to move forward into the planning process. Teachers can make parents aware of the transition and community-based activities available to the student and, by presenting positive options and the image of the student as a capable employee or community participant, help parents to move beyond previously held stereotypes or expectations. Transition-related goals and objectives should be a part of students' educational programs from elementary school onward, but during adolescence these become particularly important (and mandated by law). Families who have had experience with transition goal setting throughout the student's schooling will be more willing and able to participate in transition planning during adolescence.

In summary, the level of family participation in education has been rising since the middle of the twentieth century. Since 1975, family involvement in education and transition planning for students with disabilities has been mandated by law. Research shows that involvement improves student attitudes, attendance, and learning, and it also benefits the school and community. If begun early in the student's schooling, it is more beneficial to the student, and it helps the family prepare for the transition period. Despite these benefits, in many cases the ideal of an equal partnership between family and professionals has not been realized. The next chapter looks more closely at some of the barriers to successful family–professional collaborations.

CHAPTER 2
Barriers to Effective Family Involvement

An "uneasy relationship" is how Sonnenschein (1981) characterized the partnership between professionals and the families of students with disabilities. A partnership is a two-way street and breakdowns in collaborations between the professionals and family members can arise out of the preconceptions or actions of either or both parties.

PROFESSIONAL MISHANDLING OF FAMILIES

In the past, families were not equal partners in education for a variety of reasons (Turnbull & Turnbull, 1997), and this inequality remains to some extent today. One contributing factor to the current situation is the inaccurate or unfair set of conceptualizations held of families by professionals. Many professionals perceive families as "vulnerable clients" and view their own role in the school–home interaction as one of a "helper." In a relationship built on these assumptions, the professional is the "expert," someone who has the answers as well as the power and control to change outcomes for the family (Sonnenschein, 1981). With little consultation, the expert attempts to "fit" the family into programs (Singer & Powers, 1993). Such relationships do not lend themselves to equal partnerships or collaborative efforts.

A related perception is that of families as "patients." Professionals may view the birth of a child with a disability as an event precipitating a sequence of emotions from grieving to acceptance such as those associated with coping with the death of a loved one. Families are "labeled" as being at one point or another in this acceptance process, and often are seen as experiencing stress or anxiety because they cannot come to terms with the child's disability. As a result, the professional views the family members themselves as in need of remediation and attention. According to this view, "families are necessarily pathological because of the 'burden' imposed by raising a child with a disability" (Singer & Powers, 1993, p. 4). The professional with "this orientation stresses family problems and uses language derived from medicine in which pathology, treatment, cure and prescription are common terms. It is assumed that parents require training, need assistance to learn how to raise their children and, invariably, are distressed" (Singer & Powers, 1993, p. 5).

Yet another common perception about families is that they are responsible for their child's disabling condition. Turnbull and Turnbull (1978) reported that professionals they encountered never "came right out and said, 'You caused it,' but everything they did was based on that premise" (p. 42). Early theories regarding the etiology of certain disabilities, most notably autism, explicitly blamed parents (usually mothers) for their child's condition. Whether this perception of parental blame is grounded in fact or simply part of the mythology of disability professionals, its impact on creating partnerships is devastating. Moreover, part of the reason that this perception exists is that many parents hold feelings of guilt and harbor questions about their own culpability in their child's developmental outcomes. It is a short distance from parental feelings of guilt to professionals' assumptions of responsibility.

Professionals may subscribe to other myths about the family's ability to contribute to the planning and decision-making process. Cutler (1993) lists several such myths:

- Parents are naive laypersons who can't and shouldn't teach.

- Parents are too emotionally involved to evaluate their children.

- Parents are still obedient school pupils who should be seen and not heard. (Cutler, 1993, p. 17)

The roots of the first myth lie in the assumption that "teaching" is limited to academic subjects and is best done by experts. This belief, however, contradicts what is now known about learning. Learning and development occur throughout the day, at school, home, or elsewhere. In fact, parents spend the most time with their children and in the long run are their only consistent teachers. Of course, professionals should not expect the home environment to reproduce the school environment. Parents generally do not educate their children by giving them worksheets, for example. Educators should appreciate the fact that activities in the home are configured within the flow of the natural routine. They should help families to identify developmentally and educationally valuable opportunities in the home that could be used as learning experiences.

The second myth harkens back to perceptions about parents as victims, clients, or patients. The assumption is that until parents "work through" their grief and accept the child's disability (acceptance is implicitly defined as viewing the child as the professional does), then they cannot move past the emotional and mental barriers they have erected to contribute in a meaningful manner. This belief is inaccurate, yet pervasive.

The final myth springs as much from the system as from any particular bias individual educators may hold. School systems are complex bureaucracies that often require "insider" knowledge to navigate. Because educators are in the system, they can sometimes work their way through this maze. But too often educators feel they must step in to work the system for families, whom they regard as naive outsiders. They forget that concern for a child can spur family members to be passionate and determined advocates—and therefore very effective in their own way.

Moreover, when parents or other family members go to the school and attempt to overcome the various barriers to equal partnership, they acquire a "reputation" and are sometimes labeled as aggressive or unrealistic. One of the authors of this monograph once heard a father proclaim that "the school believes it is acceptable to have my wife cry [be helpless], but if I react with anger [respond assertively], then the meeting is ended." Some parents encountering this resistance become more strident. The cycle repeats itself and the family–professional relationship becomes increasingly confrontational and is ultimately destroyed. While families may eventually obtain at least some of what they want, their limited success is at great cost to themselves, the educators, and the student. A great many parents conclude that these confrontations are more harmful than helpful to the student and decide not to fight the system. As a result, they may not press for what they want for fear that the resulting environment will be more difficult for their child.

FAMILY MISHANDLING OF PROFESSIONALS

While professionals may at times distort the emotions felt by a family, they are right in recognizing that the birth of a child with a disability can create stress. The truth is, many children with disabilities do require more time and energy on the part of parents than do many children without disabilities. And parents may indeed go through periods of emotional turmoil. They may feel disillusioned, disappointed, frightened, frustrated, alone, vulnerable, guilty, or unfairly treated. They may also feel committed, joyful, excited, hopeful, confident, and proud. Driven by such emotions, parents may cope with their child's disability by creating unrealistic expectations (either too positive or too negative) or denying certain limitations. But such scenarios are not uncommon to parents of children without disabilities!

Some parents simply respond negatively to having a professional involved in their family life. They may not be honest with the professional (or themselves) about their feelings and expectations. Some find it difficult to admit to a professional that they do not want or are not able to take on additional responsibilities such as working with the student at home or participating in multidisciplinary team meetings (Cutler, 1993). Finally, some parents may rely too much on professionals and make unreasonable demands for attention and time.

Moreover, some parents, by necessity, must take one day at a time and have little interest in the long-term objectives that professionals bring to their attention. In truth they may be fearful of the future. Medical professionals, and sometimes educational personnel as well, may have alarmed them with dark predictions of likely outcomes for their child. Even in the 1990s, parents are frequently told at the time of the birth of their child with a disability that institutionalization is the only option they can reasonably consider. As a result, they prefer not to focus on the future.

Like educators, parents also bring inaccurate perceptions and beliefs to the school–home relationship. Cutler (1993) identified three myths about educators held by many parents:

- Educators are super experts in their field.
- Educators are totally objective.
- Educators are free agents. (p. 29)

As Cutler notes, these myths are the mirror images of the myths about parents.

Regarding the first myth, educators indeed have skills and training that enable them to work with students with disabilities and to provide answers to difficult problems and situations. They also have a large number of students, limited time, and high demands on their time. Educators are as constrained by the system as parents are and often equally frustrated. Therefore the stereotype of professionals as holding all knowledge—a stereotype perpetuated by schools and readily accepted by many parents—places undue burden on teachers and creates unrealistic expectations among parents. These expectations are often played out in unreasonable demands on the teachers' time and unfair criticism if the teacher is unable to deliver.

If families are viewed as too emotional or unobjective to be useful to the process, educators are viewed as too objective. This has been reinforced by the fact that, during their training, almost all educators became familiar with the concept of "professional distance." Parents may misinterpret the distance as a lack of sympathy. The truth is teachers are not totally objective any more than parents are totally subjective.

Lastly, many parents believe incorrectly that educators are free agents. According to Cutler (1993): "Many parents ask why, if the school personnel know a program is needed, they don't just set it up. Since it is the school's job to educate all children, parents expect that school people will do what is necessary" (pp. 35–36). What these parents fail to take into account is that, far from being free agents, teachers and educators are bound to a system that is often slow and unresponsive and does not have unlimited time, budget, or personnel. Teachers can be caught between their empathy with the family and the knowledge that advocating on behalf of the family may put at risk their friendship with colleagues, good standing with the administration, even their job. Educators may also find themselves trying to resolve an inner conflict between what they see as their responsibility to the student and their responsibility to the family. Far from being free agents, educators are in fact pulled in all directions!

BARRIERS OVERCOME: THE SUCCESSFUL PARTNERSHIP

The role of families caring for a child with disabilities is to make the best possible decisions. They therefore need information and advice from educators and other professionals. The role of the professionals is to empower families to make those decisions. When families and professionals view one another as collaborators in this way they can begin building a relationship based on mutual trust and respect. Sonnenschein (1981) identifies the following visible indicators of such a relationship:

- Information, impressions, and evaluations are promptly and openly shared.

- Collaborators are able to communicate their feelings, needs, and priorities without worrying about being labeled in a derogatory way.

- Collaborators can ask each other for help without being made to feel weak or incompetent and are able to say "I don't know" or "I don't understand" without fearing the loss of respect or credibility.

- Efforts are made to avoid the use of jargon or any practice that tends to make the other feel like an outsider. Careful attention is given to the implementation of procedures that encourage dialogue and equal sense of control. (p. 65)

Sinclair and Christenson (1991) echo these indicators in identifying five key elements of effective and respectful parent–professional interactions: (1) mutual respect for skills and knowledge; (2) honest and clear communication; (3) two-way sharing of information; (4) mutually agreed upon goals; and (5) shared planning and decision making. Like many others, these authors emphasize communication as the first step in collaboration.

In summary, both educators and families have preconceptions that can interfere with their joint collaboration. Educators may view themselves as experts and view families as distressed, subjective, and naive. Families may object to having specialists involved in their lives, or they may expect more than the specialists can reasonably deliver. The professional who really wants to help a student will try to understand the family dynamics and draw family members into the decision-making process.

CHAPTER 3
Family Systems Theory

A good special education program focuses on the individual student's unique strengths and needs—while still taking into account *the role of the student's family in its entirety.* Although it is true that "every family is unique," every family is also alike in being a dynamic "system" of interacting members. Turnbull and Turnbull (1996) quote V. Satir in characterizing family life as a mobile in which "all of the pieces, no matter what size or shape, can be grouped together and balanced by shortening or lengthening the strings attached, or rearranging the distance between the pieces" (p. 195). Satir adds, "So it is with a family. None of the family members is identical to any other; they are all different and at different levels of growth." As students and families move through the transition planning process, each member takes on new roles and responsibilities, thereby changing the delicate balance of the family mobile. Therefore, as professionals work with families and students in transition, it is important that they have a firm understanding of how family systems affect transition and vice versa, and to keep the mobile perspective in mind: "As in a mobile, you can't arrange one without thinking about the others" (Turnbull & Turnbull, 1996, p. 195).

Chapter 2 examined the various barriers to family–professional collaboration. These may make transition planning and program implementation seem like an overwhelming task. However, the "family systems" orientation presented in this chapter provides professionals with strategies for putting aside these barriers.

Family systems theory views the family as an interrelated system with unique characteristics, relationships, strengths, and needs (Turnbull & Turnbull, 1990). Viewing the family as a system means giving careful consideration to how the actions of each member affect the family as a whole (Carter & McGoldrick, 1980), and how the roles and responsibilities of each member arise out of the family's values and norms as well as the resources at their disposal (Turnbull, Barber, Behr, & Kerns, 1988). The family's most basic purpose is to ensure that its survival and developmental needs are met (Terkelson, 1980). As individual family members move through different life stages, they assume new roles and responsibilities. At these times the family must reorganize and redefine each member's roles, both in relationship to other members and to the family as a whole (Mederer & Hill, 1983; McGoldrick & Carter, 1982). This is particularly true during the transition from school to adult life, when the adolescent begins to assert new roles, responsibilities, and expectations.

Special education traditionally focused attention on the student with disabilities. Typically a special education professional expected the family (primarily the mother) to participate in the development of the IEP and then support (and perhaps even repeat at home) the school's educational strategies. This perspective emphasized the student's progress on the goals and benchmarks specified in the IEP.

In contrast, the family systems point of view is concerned with the whole family: how to involve siblings, extended family members, and parents in the student's transition program; how to gain access to the resources and networks of family and friends in order to help the student to live, work, and participate in the community; and how to gauge the impact of this major life transition upon the entire family. The difference between the traditional perspective and the family systems approach has been summarized as follows: "The application of family systems theory to special education requires fundamental changes in the answer to the following question: Who is the consumer of services delivered by special education professionals? In the past, the student has been viewed as the sole consumer. The family systems approach identifies the whole family as the consumer of services" (Turnbull & Morningstar, 1993, p. 43).

Ann and Rud Turnbull, co-directors of The Beach Center on Families and Disability, and their colleagues at this research and training center have developed a family systems framework that focuses specifically on families who have children with disabilities. The four major components of this framework are

1. Family characteristics—the descriptive elements of the family, including characteristics of the exceptionality; characteristics of the family (e.g., sizes and forms, cultural backgrounds, socioeconomic status, geographic locations); personal characteristics (e.g., health, coping styles); and special challenges (e.g., poverty, abuse). From a systems perspective, these [characteristics] can be thought of as the *input* into family interactions.

2. Family interactions—the relationships that occur among subgroups of family members on a daily and weekly basis. These relationships, the press of interaction, are responsive to individual and collective family needs.

3. Family functions—the different categories of needs the family is responsible for addressing. The purpose, or *output,* of family interaction is to produce responses to fulfill the needs associated with family functions.

4. Family life cycle—the sequence of developmental and nondevelopmental *changes* that affect families. These changes alter family characteristics (e.g., a child is born) and family functions (e.g., mother stops working outside the home, which provides more time for child-rearing but less family income). These changes, in turn, influence how the family interacts. (Turnbull & Turnbull, 1990, p. 17, italics in original)

A professional who understands the four elements of this framework should be able to find appropriate ways to include family members in transition planning, as active and equal participants.

FAMILY CHARACTERISTICS

What is your definition of a family? This seemingly straightforward question is fraught with ambiguity. How you answer depends upon the lens through which you see the world. Everyone's view is affected by cultural and social perspectives.

In the United States, the family is still frequently envisioned as two parents, with the father working full time outside the home and the mother a stay-at-home homemaker, and two or three children—all living in a house in the suburbs. However, Hanson and Carta (1996) contend that "the view of the 'nuclear' family as a 'one size fits all' pattern is giving way to a perspective that more clearly reflects the diversity of families today. Families come in all shapes and sizes" (p. 202). According to these authors, a look at television provides a more realistic picture: "single parents, blended families, extended families, foster families, and so on" (p. 202).

The overall dynamic of a family with a member with a disability depends on *family characteristics:* (a) the nature of the disability; (b) the general nature of the family; (c) the personal profiles of family members; and (d) special challenges such as poverty, abuse, and violence (Turnbull & Turnbull, 1997). Table 3.1 provides more descriptive information about these characteristics.

Changing Characteristics of Families

Hanson and Carta (1996) have identified several changes in family characteristics over the past decade. The first is the change in family composition. The authors report a study by Hernandez (1994) that projects that almost half of all Caucasian children in America born after 1980 will live in single-parent (or no-biological-parent) families; for African American children, this rate is projected to rise to 80%. The majority of these single parents are mothers.

A second changing characteristic identified by Hanson and Carta is parental employment patterns. Over 60% of all married women with children younger than 6 years old are currently in the labor force. Therefore fewer and fewer women are staying at home full time to raise their children, let alone finding the time to be active in school programs. Another trend they report is the widening income gap between less-skilled and more-skilled workers. Their data show that those with fewer skills and less education (typically, women in the role of single parents) are relegated to the bottom of the socioeconomic strata.

Special education professionals must take into account these changes in family structure when they consider the role and involvement of family members during transition. The expectation that single-parent families will be able to participate actively in all aspects of a school-oriented transition process can result in frustration and disappointment for all involved. Just being able to attend a school meeting in the middle of the workday may be a challenge for these families. Therefore those involved in transition planning need to shift their orientation to consider specifically how these families can be contributing members of the team.

Greater Diversity

The ethnic and cultural characteristics of the U.S. population are becoming increasingly diverse, with some estimates that almost one-third of the population will be people of color by the year 2010 (Harry & Kalyanpur, 1994). Addressing the needs of culturally diverse students and their families in transition planning requires reexamination of assumptions about ideal postschool adult outcomes. The traditional postschool goals for students with disabilities may not meet the needs of culturally diverse students and families including those who are Native American (Shafer & Rangasamy, 1995), African American (Sailor, 1994), Hispanic (Blackorby & Wagner, 1996), or from rural areas (Navarrete & White, 1994).

In fact, some have argued that the "cultural underpinnings of special education" (Harry & Kalyanpur, 1994, p. 145) are based upon assumptions of a dominant culture (i.e., European Protestant) that is in conflict with many other cultures. They feel the system of special education creates "threads of dissonance that often complicate even the best professional attempts at communication with parents"

(continues)

TABLE 3.1
Defining Family Characteristics

	Definition	Implications for Transition
Characteristics of the Exceptionality	Different disabilities bring unique challenges to families. How the child's specific needs affect the family may depend more upon the individual demands that a particular disability places upon the family and how the family is able to respond to these demands than upon the label or severity of the actual disability. Rather than focusing only on the disability, professionals should be aware of what the family priorities are regarding their needs related to the child's disability. Keep in mind these needs will change over the lifespan of the child and the family as a whole. In addition, professionals should be sure to focus on the contributions and strengths of the child and not solely on areas of deficit due to the disability.	• A young adult who uses a wheelchair in a rural community will be limited in his ability to get around town thereby requiring assistance from family members in order to participate in community activities. • A teenager supported by a ventilator may need in-home care from a nurse. He will need to learn self-advocacy skills in order to self-direct this care rather than relying upon his parents to do this for him.
Characteristics of the Family	Family characteristics include size and composition, cultural and ethnic identities, socioeconomic status, and geographic location. Each of these characteristics shape how the family responds to the child with a disability. Individual family characteristics can be considered to be both potential resources and limitations to how the family will cope with issues of the disability during transition. It is important that professionals have a clear understanding of the family's make up in order to support families during transition. For example, self-determination for a young person with mental retardation may be viewed differently by certain cultural groups. Professionals may misunderstand the family's lack of support for the child running the IEP meeting as not wanting to let go of the control, when in fact the child-run meeting may be counter to their cultural expectations regarding who makes decisions in the family.	• Parents of a teenager with disabilities who has older siblings may be more prepared for the issues related to transition because they have already helped their older children through this period of transition. • Hispanic families may view with suspicion any discussion about their daughter moving out of the home since this may run counter to their concept of adulthood. • A single-parent family living in poverty may need the money provided by SSI to support the family as a whole and may not want their son with disabilities to work in supported employment because of the fear of a reduction in SSI.

TABLE 3.1 *Continued.*

	Definition	Implications for Transition
Personal Characteristics of Family Members	The personal characteristics of family members can influence their relationship with their child as well as with transition professionals. Physical health, mental health, and coping styles are all examples of personal characteristics that can affect how professionals and family members interact. It is important to identify how individual characteristics of family members will support or detract from collaboration with professionals. For example, if the mother is undergoing a serious illness, her ability to be actively involved in transition may be diminished. Understanding how individual families cope with the stress associated with transition will assist professionals in providing effective support.	• For some families, relying on social support networks is the preferred method of coping with stress. Job developers therefore should encourage the involvement of extended family members and friends in assisting in job searches. • For families who cope with stress by "planning one day at a time," discussions about transition will be extremely difficult. Therefore, professionals should consider how they can help families to begin planning earlier and in smaller steps so that they are not overwhelmed by the planning process.
Special Challenges	Some families face serious challenges such as poverty, drug and alcohol abuse, and exposure to high levels of violence. These issues are very complex and often lead to multiple risks for families with adolescents with disabilities. The extreme stresses of these special challenges create chaos within family systems. Families struggling daily with issues such as being able to feed their children, domestic violence, and drug abuse may be incapable of planning for the future for their teenager with disabilities.	• Families with multiple challenges will require more than just school-based services. While the focus during transition planning is typically on the young adult with disabilities, professionals will need to consider how to support the family in meeting their complex needs.

Note. Compiled from *Families, Professionals, and Exceptionality: A Special Partnership* (3rd ed.), by A. P. Turnbull and H. R. Turnbull, 1997, Upper Saddle River, NJ: Merrill/Prentice Hall and from "Family and Professional Interaction," by A. P. Turnbull and M. E. Morningstar, 1993, in *Instruction of Students with Severe Disabilities* (4th ed.) edited by M. Snell, New York: Merrill.

(Harry & Kalyanpur p. 148). For instance, special education's emphasis on independence and individual achievement may cause conflict for many families from different cultures with differing values. When professional and parental values conflict, then the parents' traditional trust in authority is undermined. Under these circumstances, parents may appear to defer to professionals, but they may not cooperate with the professional recommendations or respond to requests for parental involvement. School professionals, then, often misinterpret this lack of parental involvement as disinterest, apathy, or neglect (Harry, 1992; Harry, Allen, & McLaughlin, 1995).

The mainstream U.S. beliefs about success, mirrored in the IDEA transition outcomes for students with disabilities, are often in direct conflict with the values and beliefs of some cultural groups. While professional focus on the transition experiences of culturally diverse students appears to be increasing (Navarrete & White, 1994), the research on culturally diverse populations of students and families in transition is still relatively small. For example, a recent review of 12 studies examining families in transition found that only half of these studies even reported participants' ethnicity; in the ones that did report, the ethnic percentage was typically small (Blue-Banning, 1997). When studies do specifically focus on postschool outcomes for specific groups of culturally diverse students with disabilities, the results are discouraging:

Hispanic Students

The National Longitudinal Transition Survey (NLTS) measured transition outcomes for Hispanic youth and found significantly lower rates of employment and independent living than those of their white peers (Blackorby & Wagner, 1996). In addition, some have argued that the concepts inherent in self-determination (i.e., self-advocacy, individual autonomy, and control) are antithetical to traditional values of Hispanic families and therefore could lead to conflict (Turnbull & Turnbull, 1996).

Native American Students

Students with and without disabilities from an Apache reservation in Arizona equally experienced poverty, unemployment, disenfranchisement, and lack of opportunity. The researchers Shafer and Rangasamy (1995) concluded that the explicit IDEA transition goals of employment and independent living were both elusive and in many instances culturally inappropriate. The values inherent in transition, such as independence, individualization, and competition, were in direct conflict with Native American values of cooperation, interdependence, and communal responsibility (Clay, 1992).

African American Students

A recent review of service delivery for African Americans with developmental disabilities in Kansas indicated that an estimated 86% to 94% were unserved by adult agencies (Sailor, 1994). Large numbers of African American young adults with disabilities are therefore completely cut off from formal services and supports necessary for successful adult life. This is particularly noteworthy given recent indications that African American students with more significant levels of mental retardation are overrepresented in special education services, similar to their African American peers with more mild mental retardation (Harry, Grenot-Scheyer, et al., 1995). These two trends indicate that African American students are more likely to be identified with disabilities but are less likely to be served by community adult agencies.

Clearly, the issues surrounding cultural diversity and transition are complex. Despite increasing ethnicity in the United States, many school professionals still have limited direct experiences with cultural traditions other than their own (Harry, Grenot-Scheyer, et al., 1995). Those most closely associated with the problems and barriers to family–professional interactions have emphasized the importance of going beyond multicultural education and developing "cultural reciprocity" as a cornerstone of educational services (Harry & Kalyanpur, 1994). Moving toward cultural reciprocity will require professionals to reconsider values and assumptions inherent in their own belief systems. The good news is that researchers, families, and others concerned with issues related to cultural diversity have begun the process of addressing ways to do this. Table 3.2 provides some steps for increasing professionals' cultural competence and opening up a dialogue between parents and professionals.

TABLE 3.2

Steps to Achieving Cultural Competence and Reciprocity

General Strategies	Source
1. Ask rather than make assumptions about what language is spoken at home and by which members.	Harry, Grenot-Scheyer, et al., 1995
2. Set goals that take into account the cultural and family norms for personal and social development; this is particularly important with regard to employment and independent living goals.	
3. Develop a clear understanding of the cultural interpretations of the disability. Many cultures differ in the meanings attributed to the disability. These views may affect how the family copes.	
4. Respect the child-rearing practices of the culture and do not place blame on the family for ways in which those practices differ from those of the mainstream.	
5. Ensure that parents have access to all sources of information including advocacy groups, and that materials explaining rights and responsibilities are made available in the native language or through personalized explanations by speakers of the family's language.	
6. Enhance self-awareness by understanding who you are from a variety of perspectives including your family origins and your beliefs, biases, and behaviors. Be aware that your beliefs and values may be very different from those of the families you work with.	Turnbull & Turnbull, 1997
7. Enhance culture-specific awareness by learning about different cultural groups in terms of child-rearing practices and family patterns. Be careful not to stereotype but become familiar with the general traditions, customs, and values of the families in your community.	
8. Enhance culture-generic awareness by identifying values and practices that are found in all cultures. This is a way to develop some common ground when working with families from different cultures.	

(continues)

TABLE 3.2 *Continued.*

General Strategies	Source
9. Enhance cultural issues related to the disability by understanding how cultural views influence the definition and meaning of the disability and therefore the family–professional roles, communication patterns, and expectations and anticipated outcomes.	
10. Establish alliances with culturally diverse families by taking a personalized approach to working with the family.	
11. Develop outcomes and strategies for facilitating transition to adulthood that promote self-esteem, community interdependence, and inclusion.	Shafer & Rangasamy, 1995
12. Improve the multicultural competence of team members: • Provide opportunities for team members to learn how the world views and values of other cultures might differ from their own. • Provide opportunities for team members to learn about intercultural communication, including nonverbal communication. • Subscribe to resources that focus on multicultural issues including journals and internet discussion groups. • Gather feedback from families regarding their satisfaction with special education services. 13. Expose culturally diverse students and families to a variety of role models and resources: • Subscribe to magazines that highlight culturally diverse role models and use these in various content areas. • Develop mentor programs with role models of color in the community.	Navarrete & White, 1994

Cultural issues are not, however, simply a great divide! Luera (1994) identified four roles that, in spite of cultural differences, parents seem to perform across cultures:

Parents as Nurturers

Parents form an important nurturing relationship with their child. Parents of a child with special needs must often learn and understand the unique ways in which their child requests and responds to nurturing. This role, while it may be taken largely for granted, is the primary role for parents and thus critically important to the child.

Parents as Models for Family Roles, Knowledge, Customs, and Traditions

Children learn about families, their culture, customs, and traditions by being a part of the family. Parents are the primary role models for teaching children how to behave in daily life situations and introducing them to the customs and traditions that are important to the family.

Parents as Guides for Their Child

Virtually all parents want their child to develop into an accepted, valued member of the community in which they live. While different methods for guiding are used, and variations of acceptable behavior exist in cultures, the desired outcome is that their child behaves in a manner that is appropriate to the social situation.

Parents as Teachers Who Assist the Child in Learning to Problem-Solve

Problem-solving (and decision-making) skills are typically learned by watching one's parents and other valued adults solve problems and make decisions. Chapter 5 provides suggestions for promoting self-determination, including problem solving.

Finally, Luera (1994) identified three common parenting goals that cross cultures:

1. Desire to be effective in parenting;
2. Security for the child;
3. Success of the child in functioning as societal member.

FAMILY INTERACTIONS

Family interactions are the process by which the system's inputs (i.e., the individual and collective characteristics that make up the family) are turned into outputs, or the things the family does (Turnbull & Turnbull, 1997). In other words how the various members interact both individually and within smaller subgroups of the family determines how they mitigate any special challenges and use their resources to their benefits. These interactions that vitalize a family are like the heat needed to leaven and bake bread. Without the heat, bread would be nothing more than an inert ball of flour, water, and yeast. Moreover, in the case of families, the process is reciprocal; how a family interacts also affects the characteristics of the family (Figure 3.1).

To collaborate successfully with families during transition planning, professionals need to consider carefully how the members interact and the differing roles that they play. Two key elements of family interactions are the changes in the role of the student with disabilities within the family and the part played by siblings in that student's life.

The Changing Role of the Student

Professional understanding of the different roles of family members is especially critical during transition, a time when society expects young adults to assume more and more autonomy in making decisions and in taking responsibility for their actions (Lichtenstein, 1998). Increased independence from family may not be the case for families with young adults with disabilities. The major life roles typically assumed by teenagers (e.g., having an after-school job, driving a car, opening a checking account) may be significantly delayed, if they occur at all. In fact, a family may see no end to their involvement in their child's life and quite often must become more engaged in the postschool period due to the lack of community adult services and supports (Brotherson, Backus, Summers, & Turnbull, 1986; Ferguson, Ferguson, & Jones, 1988; Hanley-Maxwell, Whitney-Thomas, & Pogoloff, 1995).

Perhaps what is needed is a reconsideration of "adulthood." Research indicates that students with disabilities overwhelmingly desire to continue their close involvement with their families, who give them both concrete and emotional support (Lichtenstein, 1993; Morningstar, 1995). In their case the definition of adulthood could be revised to take into account the preference of the young person to

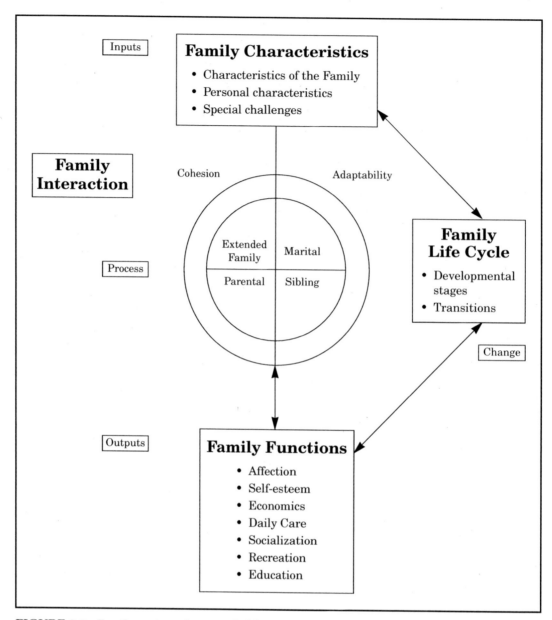

FIGURE 3.1. Family systems framework. *Note.* Adapted from *Families, Professionals, and Exceptionality: A Special Partnership* (3rd ed.), by A. P. Turnbull and H. R. Turnbull, 1997, Upper Saddle River, NJ: Merrill/Prentice Hall.

maintain an *interdependent relationship* with the family (Turnbull & Turnbull, 1997) and the community (Ferguson & Ferguson, 1993). Adulthood might then be defined by the changing roles and responsibilities *within* the family setting (McGoldrick & Carter, 1982; Super, 1990; Turnbull et al., 1988). Some cultures would even accept this definition for all young adults, not just those with disabilities. In fact, in some cultures, moving out on one's own might be viewed as a disgrace to the family (Turnbull & Turnbull, 1997). Therefore, as educational professionals embark on the process of transition planning, they must be careful to consider the preferences of both the student and family regarding this level of independence and separation.

This issue has taken on new urgency with the 1997 reauthorization of IDEA. Schools must now notify the family of the transfer of rights when the student with disabilities reaches the legal age of majority. The student becomes the lead decision maker. This new regulation has been hailed as opening the door for all students with disabilities to take greater responsibility for their transition planning and to encourage schools to begin self-determination skills training.

Certainly students with disabilities who are not self-determined will lack the skills necessary to achieve successful adult outcomes (Wehmeyer & Schwartz, 1997). Indeed the lack of self-determination may be one of the critical factors leading to poor postschool outcomes for students with disabilities (Wehmeyer, Agran, & Hughes, 1998). But self-determination should be considered from a family systems perspective and not exclusively in the legalistic "age of majority" terms of the IDEA.

Although a sizeable body of literature on self-determination models and research now exists (Field & Hoffman, 1994; Martin & Marshall, 1996; Powers, Singer, & Sowers, 1996; Sands & Wehmeyer, 1996; Van Reusen et al., 1994; Wehmeyer, 1998; Wehmeyer, Agran, & Hughes, 1998), not enough focuses on the role that families play in supporting decision making and self-determination, a role that varies from culture to culture (Turnbull & Turnbull, 1996).

Data from a recent study indicate that students with a range of disabilities are making a variety of decisions about their lives (Morningstar, 1995). Over 70 students with disabilities interviewed identified making simple decisions ranging from deciding what to wear to having sexual relationships. Yet students often seemed to lack any systematic method for making good decisions. Some students talked about the role of their families in helping them to make decisions, but this family involvement appeared to be informal at best. It was clear from this research that students were seeking autonomy in making certain kinds of decisions, but they were also relying on family support for others (Gallivan-Felon, 1994; Hanley-Maxwell et al., 1995; Turnbull & Turnbull, 1997).

Certainly parents play an important role in supporting self-determination (Brotherson et al., 1988; Powers et al., 1996; Turnbull & Turnbull, 1997), yet they often experience obstacles. Powers and others (1996) have identified four such barriers: (a) uncertainty about how much self-determination they can expect from their children with disabilities; (b) uncertainty about the strategies they could use to encourage self-determination; (c) concern about allowing their children to take risks that will result in harm; and (d) multiple challenges (e.g., poverty, unemployment, health problems) that may prevent them from promoting self-determination. For special education professionals, an important task is providing a variety of ways to help parents to enhance and promote self-determination for their children with disabilities (see chapter 5 for additional suggestions).

The issues of decision making and self-determination are a critical part of a family-centered approach to transition planning. A better understanding of family-centered practices has emerged from the early childhood literature (Dunst, Johnson, Trivette, & Hamby, 1991; Bailey, Buysse, Smith, & Elam, 1992; Shelton, Jeppson, & Johnson, 1989; Turbiville, Turnbull, Garland, & Lee, 1996). But much of the major work done on self-determination has been concentrated within secondary special education and has focused more explicitly on student rather than family supports. What is needed is to bring together family-centered and community-centered practices within the context of student self-determination (Morningstar, Turnbull, & Turnbull, 1995).

Professionals need to increase the emphasis on self-determination in family-centered and culturally appropriate ways, even during early childhood years (Brotherson, Cook, Cunconan-Lahr, & Wehmeyer, 1995). They should provide opportunities for students to express their preferences for activities, and to self-assess their strengths and needs. Family roles need to be reconceptualized to complement this increased emphasis on student autonomy and decision making. Parents and extended family must have opportunities to collaborate with professionals as well as with their child in collective decision making.

The Role of Siblings in Transition

A second issue related to family interactions is the potential role that siblings can play in transition planning. Siblings often provide the very first experience in peer relationships for a child with a disability (Powell & Gallagher, 1993). They can also be instrumental in introducing the child to the neighborhood, school, and larger community and then provide ongoing support in these environments. In later years siblings may take on the responsibility of providing care or coordination of services, particularly as their parents age (Selzer, Krauss, & Janicki, 1994). For example, in a recent longitudinal study of the transition experiences of young adults supported by medical technology (i.e., ventilators and/or gastrostomy tubes), several mothers indicated that an older sibling was to take responsibility for the well-being of the younger one who had the disabilities (Morningstar, Turnbull, Reichard, & Umbarger, 1998).

How much responsibility siblings will need to take varies from family to family. But certainly their role depends upon family expectations and the relationships they develop over the years with the sibling with disabilities. Therefore it is advantageous for professionals to have a sense of these sibling relationships and to encourage and support the involvement of siblings during transition planning.

The impact of a young adult with disabilities upon siblings depends upon many factors, but it is a fallacy to assume that this effect is always negative. Suffice to say there are probably good and bad elements, just as there are with all sibling relationships, regardless of the personal characteristic of having a disability.

FAMILY FUNCTIONS

A basic assumption of family systems theory is that systems strive to maintain equilibrium. This assumption can be applied to the family system as well. Turnbull, Summers, and Brotherson (1986) identified seven primary functions that families perform in order to meet the individual and collective needs of their members. These are

1. Economic—generating income and handling family finances, paying bills, earning allowances, and handling insurance matters.

2. Daily care—purchasing food, preparing meals, providing health and maintenance care, maintaining the home, providing transportation, and taking general safety measures.

3. Recreation—going on vacations, developing and participating in hobbies or clubs, and setting aside everyday demands.

4. Socialization—developing individual and collective friendships and social skills, and engaging in social activities.

5. Self-definition—establishing self-identify and self-image, awareness of personal strengths and weaknesses, and feelings of belonging and acceptance.

6. Affection—developing intimate personal relationships, expressing one's sexuality, giving and receiving nurturance and love, and expressing emotions.

7. Educational and vocational—participating in school-related activities, continuing education for family adults, doing homework, providing for career development, and developing a work ethic. (Turnbull & Morningstar, 1993, p. 49)

While each of these seven categories of family functions are distinct, they are not mutually exclusive; the problems and benefits from one dimension affect other functions that in turn influence the interactions and roles of the family members (Turnbull & Turnbull, 1996). For example, Morningstar and colleagues (1998) describe a situation in which a single mother working full time reported that her daughter with severe cerebral palsy graduated from school and made the transition to an adult service agency for daytime employment. However, the agency refused to tube-feed her daughter due to state regulations that define this as a skilled nursing function. Therefore, in order for her daughter to remain at the agency for the entire day (and meet her educational and vocational "function") the mother had to leave her job and go to feed her daughter, thereby disrupting her work day and potentially threatening her ability to provide a basic economic "function" for the family.

School and transition professionals typically concentrate their energies on helping students to accomplish specific activities that would fall within the educational and vocational category of family functions. However, this narrow focus may exclude their involvement in supporting the student and family in other functions that may be more urgent. Professionals involved with the transition planning process may best support the family and student by recognizing the complex and interrelated needs of families (Turnbull & Morningstar, 1993).

This recognition helps to bring about a necessary balance between professional expectations and family priorities during transition. For instance, on the one hand, we know that families and students who begin the transition planning process early achieve better outcomes (Brotherson et al., 1986; McNair & Rusch, 1991). On the other hand, some families and students report feeling pressure from schools to begin the formal transition process before they are ready (Morningstar, 1995; Morningstar, Lattin, & Steinle, 1995). If schools do not determine the goals of students and families, they may in their zeal provide early transition planning that is unwelcome.

Transition after all is only one of many functions that families address and may, in fact, not be a priority at the time when professionals think it should begin. In addition, professionals should be wary of pushing families to think about the future to the exclusion of other aspects of their life. For example, many parents have described feeling pressure from early intervention programs to work constantly with their child to make more substantial gains (Turnbull, Turnbull, & Blue-Banning, 1994). This problem could also occur during transition; that is, families might feel pressured to participate in a planning process that does not meet their preferences and concerns.

Clearly special education professionals are faced with the challenge of providing transition planning and services early enough to meet the complex needs of students with disabilities and their families while allowing family members to maintain a balance among their myriad of roles. Professionals must ensure that students are prepared for adult life without placing undue burdens on them and their families. Hanley-Maxwell, Pogloff, and Whitney-Thomas (1998) describe this balance in the following way: "Families are urged to take the leadership role in their child's transition process. Perhaps by utilizing the best practices for including families, families will become the center of the process regardless of whether they are capable or choose to assume a traditional leadership role. . . . Becoming the center of the process can be explained by visualizing the family as the center of the universe with professionals, agencies, and informal support systems revolving around the family, providing support when needed" (p. 246).

FAMILY LIFE CYCLE

The transition of young people with disabilities from school to adult life relates specifically to the fourth element in the family systems orientation: the family life cycle. This framework is based on the notion that change takes place in a predictable sequence over a family's lifespan (Mederer & Hill, 1983). Children are born; they go to school with their friends; they get a job after school delivering newspapers; they learn to drive; they graduate from high school; they go to college; and they get jobs and live on their own. These life events mark the changing roles, responsibilities, and needs of individual family members, and these all have an impact upon the family as a whole.

The life cycle theory is helpful in that it provides a picture of how families change and adapt as they move through time. But for the family with a child with a disability, the life cycle perspective may not provide enough information, particularly during transition to adulthood. The life cycle is based on age-linked markers of developmental growth that signify the family member's achievement of greater levels of independence. As mentioned earlier, families of children with disabilities often do not experience the cues that lead to the shifting of responsibility from parents to the young adult with a disability. They cannot always rely on the natural process of change and must instead deliberately plan for their child's movement into adulthood (Brotherson et al., 1986; Hanley-Maxwell et al., 1995; McNair & Rusch, 1991). If they have not laid sufficient groundwork for the transition to adulthood, they may delay this stage in the life cycle and make it more difficult to achieve. Federal legislation now recognizes that the shift to adulthood may not be synonymous with movement into the workforce. The federal interpretation of transition has expanded beyond employment (Will, 1984) to include community life adjustment (Halpern, 1985; Sailor, Anderson, Halvorsen, Doering, Filler, & Goetz, 1989), quality of life (Halpern, 1993), and self-determination (Ward & Halloran, 1993).

In reality, however, most families (i.e., families of all types) often do not go through the "normal" phases of family development at "normal" times (McGoldrick & Carter, 1982). In addition, the transitional periods they are in may last much longer than life cycle theory implies. Rather than long and enduring periods of stability followed by brief periods of disorganization and reorganization, transition may more typically occur over an extended period of time (Mederer and Hill, 1983). For many families, life stages seem to merge into one another without sharp breaks in between. The families undergo a slow and continual disruption of their established patterns of interactions, and new roles gradually emerge. A smooth and successful transition therefore can take place over a long period of time with a gradual replacement of established roles, responsibilities, and interactions.

Current policy initiatives such as IDEA have continued to focus on a fixed definition of transition in which preparation for the future seems to start at age 14 and stop at 21. This, of course, conflicts with the growing consensus among researchers that transition is a gradual time of change that may continue well past the age period delineated by IDEA. The process of making transitions, in fact, may require many different preparations to ensure the gradual movement toward successful community living (Brotherson & Spillers, 1989). Therefore, it is essential that professionals re-evaluate the age-segregated service delivery model as it currently stands.

Another essential element missing from the federal definitions is the impact of transition on the entire family. A successful transition should not be considered exclusively in terms of placement of the student with a disability but should include the entire family's well-being. Perhaps transition to adulthood could borrow concepts from early intervention policy and research (Summers et al., 1990). Early intervention professionals are now required to identify expected outcomes for both the child with a disability and the family. Support programs then are designed by what the family identifies as the most important outcomes for their child and the family as a whole. If transition used the same framework, it would likewise be family centered rather than focusing only on the needs of the student as the law currently does.

In summary, an expanded definition of transition must include more than the static view of a transfer of services for an individual with disabilities from school to an adult service system. To be effective, transition must be considered from the perspective of the family as a whole and the overall needs of all its members. The characteristics of families have changed in recent decades, and educators must be sensitive to the demands of single parenting, the widening income gap between skilled and unskilled labor, and the growing cultural diversity in the United States. They must consider how the family changes as a student becomes an adult, and they must evaluate the relationship between the student and siblings. They must realize that family members have different functions and that changes in one affect the others. Finally, they must remember that a smooth transition is the result of gradual changes to the family system over an extended period of time, even though the law recognizes only the ages 14 to 21 as the transition period.

Educators working with families that include young adults with disabilities must remember that transition is a process rather than an outcome. In this way they can focus on how families successfully achieve their desired outcomes over the long haul. They need to keep in mind that they may be able to provide excellent support to families and students, but their role is time-limited. They will not be there to support the student and family upon graduation from high school. Therefore, they must pay careful attention to how they can meet the specific transition needs of the student and the family, as well as foster skills and attitudes that will last over time.

CHAPTER 4

Family Involvement in Transition Assessment and Planning

A critical element of any successful transition program is the individual's functional assessment information upon which future employment, living, recreational and social, and community integration plans are based. Clark (1998), in a book in the same series as this text, provided an extensive treatment of the importance of assessments to successful transition, as well as steps to implementing such assessments. The purpose of this chapter is not to describe transition planning, per se, but instead to provide information on involving parents and family members in the planning process.

Hanley-Maxwell and colleagues (1998) noted that despite the clear mandate in the IDEA for family involvement in the educational planning process, research indicates that families too often remain passive participants in transition planning. As these authors suggested, this is unfortunate because research also indicates that family involvement is one of only a few transition practices empirically linked with transition success (Kohler, 1993). Family involvement in transition planning is critical for many reasons. Actively involving parents and other family members as equal partners in the planning process builds the true partnership discussed as important in the first chapter. Families who are involved in transition planning are more likely to become involved in aspects of transition program implementation as well. Furthermore, as has often been noted, family members hold a wealth of information about the student, such as interests, preferences, and instructional needs, and will likely be the student's primary support provider after graduation. It is little wonder that parental input into the transition planning process can be viewed as a quality indicator of successful transition programs (Sale, Metzler, Everson, & Moon, 1991; Stineman, Morningstar, Bishop, & Turnbull, 1993).

Barriers to meaningful family involvement in transition planning include those discussed in chapter 2. Stineman and colleagues (1993) identified several such barriers, including professionals' perceptions, families' past negative experiences with professionals, limited and conflicting expectations, family stress during times of transition, and the lack of opportunity to participate. Hanley-Maxwell and others (1998) identified parental lack of knowledge about their rights, the processes and procedures of the educational system, and systemic policies as barriers, as well as power relationships within the school and communication problems. Again, to reiterate the message from previous chapters, the key to successful parental and family involvement in transition, including transition planning, is a commitment to forming active school–home partnerships in which family members have an equal voice in the transition process, and whose values and opinions are respected and wants and needs are addressed.

BUILDING MEANINGFUL FAMILY INVOLVEMENT

Learning to Listen

Hanley-Maxwell and colleagues (1998) had two pieces of advice for professionals seeking to build meaningful family involvement in transition planning: *listen* and *invite*. In attempting to fulfill the expectations inherent in the role of "expert," the professional is often tempted to act, that is, state an opinion, design a plan, determine a strategy, implement an action plan, determine an outcome, and so forth. Yet the transition planning process needs to begin with another action: listening. Learning to listen to family needs, concerns, opinions, and preferences, including student interests and preferences, is a challenge to many educators. Doing so in a manner that supports active participation, rather than just leading to propagation of the "helper" role discussed in chapter 2, is especially difficult. The values inherent in effective person-centered planning (see Clark, 1998) are applicable to virtually any transition planning circumstance and constitute effective practices for "learning to listen."

Stineman and colleagues (1993) suggested that person-centered transition planning should embody the values listed in Table 4.1. While it is not the purpose of this chapter to deal extensively with the "how to" of person-centered planning, several aspects of these values warrant consideration:

First, the transition planning process is one that must be centered on student and family preferences and interests. This is consistent with the intent in the IDEA, discussed previously, that transition services must be individualized. Given that the family is the primary support for students throughout the transition period, and often well into adulthood (particularly for students with disabilities), it is a mistake to consider student interests, preferences, and needs as completely distinct or separate from family preferences and needs. Of course, at times tension may arise between student self-direction and family involvement, but this does not mean that family exclusion is necessary in order to promote student involvement (Turnbull et al., 1996; Turnbull & Turnbull, 1996; Wehmeyer & Sands, 1998). In fact, Morningstar, Turnbull, and Turnbull (1995) found that students strongly believe that families play many essential roles in helping them to plan for their future, including

- Making sure students stayed in high school;
- Planning for and helping them to pay for college;

TABLE 4.1
Values of Person Centered Transition Planning

PERSON CENTERED TRANSITION PLANNING:
Is based upon individual and family preferences.
Focuses on the positive contributions of the individual and family.
Results in solutions that are based in the community.
Illuminates as many options for choice-making as possible.
Encourages visioning, dreaming, and great expectations.

Note. Adapted from "Role of Families in Transition Planning for Young Adults with Disabilities: Toward a Method of Person-Centered Planning," by R. M. Stineman, M. E. Morningstar, B. Bishop, and H. R. Turnbull, 1993, *Journal of Vocational Rehabilitation, 3*(2).

- Helping them to move out on their own;
- Helping them to find a job. (p. 254)

Stineman and colleagues (1993) caution against a too-common practice in transition planning that can essentially mitigate against family and student interests and needs: the practice of limiting options to what program is available or what the system will allow. Such Hobson's choices are too frequent in educational practices and undermine the creation of partnerships by artificially limited options, ignoring the importance of individualized preferences and needs, and curtailing the vision-creating process.

A second value of person-centered transition planning that Stineman and others (1993) highlight is the community focus of such activities. Person-centered planning has a community inclusion bias. Transition services support the movement from school to, in essence, the community. Again, there is an all-too-familiar tendency to construe transition outcomes in terms of programs and facilities, without a concurrent consideration of how those services might affect the quality of a student's life (Halpern, 1993; Halpern and Wehmeyer, 1998). Family involvement in transition should include involvement in planning all aspects of the student's life, from employment to postsecondary education to living arrangement, and should focus on life in the community, not on facilities.

Hutchins and Renzaglia (1998) developed a tool to assist in the process of "listening" to families in relation to transition employment outcomes. Their systematic process, the "Family Vocational Interview," could, undoubtedly, be applied to other transition areas as well. They suggest using the interview "as a guide for communicating with family members and exploring their concerns and issues related to current and future vocational instruction and experiences" (p. 72). However, practitioners should be cautious not to use an instrument such as the "Family Vocational Interview" as the sole "proof" of family involvement or the exclusive means of determining family interests and needs. They should instead consider such tools, as suggested by the authors, as steps toward greater communication. The following list by Hutchins and Renzaglia provides the basic objectives of the interview process:

- Determine the family's goals and visions for, and attitudes toward, current and future vocational options for the student.

- Elicit family discussion of the student's school- or community-based work experiences and preferences.

- Identify areas in which student requires support such as daily living, mobility, and communication and which affect vocational preparation, and ways in which the family provides the support.

- Determine how families prefer to communicate with potential employers and other transition or vocational personnel.

- Determine transportation needs, options, and preferences of family members.

- Elicit family preferences concerning wages, benefits, working conditions, and other factors that influence employment selections.

Educators should also keep in mind that parents sometimes hold unspoken and often intangible concerns and worries, about a variety of topics including safety, sex, and social contacts: Will my child be safe out in the community? What if someone tries to take advantage of my daughter (or son) sexually? Will my son have friends? These legitimate concerns can become barriers to successful transition planning if the climate is not one in which parents are comfortable communicating. When educators sense that there are unspoken issues, they should encourage parents to discuss how they feel about a particular course of action as well as their concerns about the student's transition to adulthood.

Hutchins and Renzaglia provided other suggestions that would enhance family participation. For example, this participation should be ongoing and longitudinal in nature and should begin when the student enters adolescence. Family circumstances, needs, and priorities will change over the course of the transition years. Transition teachers should aim to establish an open relationship with parents and family members in which information about these changing needs are gathered in less structured and formal ways. It may be useful to establish a systematic process that on at least an annual basis ensures that newly emerging needs, changing circumstances, and shifting priorities are not inadvertently missed.

Hanley-Maxwell and colleagues (1998) identify an important distinction that should be considered when "listening" to parent needs, interests, and preferences: The process should not be undertaken so much for gathering information but for exchanging information. When decisions are made unilaterally, the decision maker gathers all the information, then acts on it in a manner consistent with personal priorities, interests, and needs. Such a model is, however, inconsistent if not antithetical to collaborative decision making and the partnership process. It is true that the teacher (or transition specialist) will be responsible for organizing all the information necessary, but the students, parents, and other family members should be key players in the decision-making process, and information should flow both to and from the school. Under these conditions, family members will feel better prepared and, presumably, more empowered to serve as equal partners in the planning process.

Another aspect of learning to listen is recognizing what to listen for. Family members often communicate wants, needs, interests, and past events by telling stories and anecdotes about their child or young adult. It is essential therefore that professionals ask questions of families in ways that allow them to answer in their own words, rather than mirroring the jargon and phrases that are second nature to professionals. The transition professionals need to have "conversations" with families as a way to gather information. If they let families take the lead and they listen carefully, professionals can elicit rich and insightful information as well as develop more collaborative relationships with families.

This is not to say that parents and family members must be held responsible for collecting all the information necessary to make effective transition decisions. As Clark (1998) illustrated, transition planning requires a variety of sources of information, including traditional standardized assessments of interests and aptitudes, work-sample and work–community site observations information, surveys of students' natural environments, situational assessments, and student self-report indices. It is not the responsibility of family members to conduct such assessments, but the outcomes of such processes should be communicated to parents and other family members in such a manner as to be understandable. The family can then add that information to their own knowledge of the student to make well-informed decisions. Clark also identified other sources of data, including medical appraisals and evaluations and parent self-report measures, that can be collected by the parent or family member. Turnbull and Turnbull (1997) likewise suggested that one means of ensuring collaboration in evaluation is for schools to rely more heavily on authentic assessments and to have family members participate actively in that process and in portfolio development.

Inviting Involvement

The second practice highlighted by Hanley-Maxwell and colleagues (1998) to promote active family involvement in transition planning was to *invite* participation. Like listening, inviting seems to be a relatively simple action. The IDEA mandates that school districts contact parents about the need for an IEP meeting, set a date, time, and location that is convenient for everyone on the team (including the parent or family member), and invite all members of the IEP team. In reality, these mandates too often become bureaucratic, administrative processes that "inform" parents of the time of a meeting, convenient or not, with the major purpose of the "invitation" to document compliance with this mandate. It may be easy to assume that parents and family members are aware of transition-related planning and feel empowered to participate as meaningful partners, but the reality is often otherwise. Many parents become disenfranchised from their child's education planning early in the process as a result of the myths, expectations, and stereotypes discussed earlier, and will not become active partners again unless teachers and transition specialists reach out and invite them into the process.

Professionals should also consider the role that siblings, extended family members, and friends might play in transition planning. Typically IEP meetings include only parents (and most often just the mother). However, extending the invitation to include those in the student's social support network is particularly worthwhile. The student's network of family and friends will be the primary source of support after leaving school (Morningstar, 1995). Therefore professionals would be wise to identify and then invite both immediate and extended family members to participate in the transition process.

Halvorsen and others (1989) suggested several strategies for reaching out to parents. The first, a parent interview, is similar to that discussed earlier. Done well (i.e., through person-centered methods), such an interview can serve the dual purposes of soliciting information upon which to base transition plans and communicating to parents that they are a welcome, important part of the planning process. Schools can organize parent meetings that bring parents together for support purposes and which provide information. Such meetings can be primarily social or educational. As an example of the latter, the Iowa Department of Education, as a part of their transition system change process, developed several parent and student inservice packages that they distributed to regional education agencies. The agencies in turn invited parents and students to workshops ranging from two hours to one day on topics that included IDEA and the transition services mandate, due process, and self-advocacy and self-determination. A primary intent of this process was to provide parents and other family members with the information they needed from the time their child began the transition process. Berry and Hardman (1998) identified six areas of transition planning in which parents and family members need such information and training:

    (a) the components of effective secondary and transition programs;
    (b) the characteristics of adult service programs;
    (c) criteria for evaluating postschool services and supports;
    (d) possible service alternatives;
    (e) the current status of services in their local community; and
    (f) the identification of innovative programs. (p. 232)

Job fairs for students and families are another commonly used way of informing family members of employment options in their community. Halvorsen and colleagues (1989) also suggested inviting family members on site visits to local work and living providers and settings to enable them to learn more about the options available to their family. These are just a few of the ways in which families can be "invited" to become meaningful participants. One word of caution, however: What works for one family may not work for others; therefore schools need to offer a range of options for family information about transition. In addition to the methods described above, other ways to support families' informational needs include written brochures, parent workshops, person-centered planning, home visits, transition fairs for students and families, and parent-to-parent mentorships.

In far too many circumstances, schools waste a potentially valuable resource: the parents and family members of the students. The implementation of effective transition programs, with the requisite community-based learning, transportation needs, and community and business involvement, may place additional stresses on the limited resources available to schools. In an effective school–home partnership, families can be encouraged to advocate for additional resources, community support, or other needed changes. For example, Lubetkin (1996) described how an elementary school in an impoverished urban area enlisted the support of the parents in the community to address safety issues and in the process created a strong and mutually beneficial advocacy relationship with parents who, up to that point, had been largely uninvolved.

While the fulcrum upon which much of the transition planning process rests is the IEP meeting, it is a mistake to view transition planning as a one-time or even annual event. Such planning should be ongoing. As such, enlisting family members as advocates in efforts that will enhance the transition program—such as increasing the number of or variability in community-based work training settings; starting, increasing, or enhancing adult community-based services such as supported employment services; or planning and advocating for more flexible school policies that would support community-based learning—will benefit the school, build stronger school–family partnerships, and better prepare the family members to help plan the student's future.

McDonnell, Mathot-Buckner, and Ferguson (1996) provide a global approach to encouraging parents to become active participants in the transition planning process. Table 4.2 summarizes each of the four steps that they recommend. Such a process provides a "concentrated effort to develop strategies that promote and support active [parent] participation in transition planning" (Berry & Hardman, 1998, p. 236).

COMING TOGETHER FOR THE IEP MEETING

Despite the fact that transition assessment and planning should be year-round activities, the focal point for this process is, almost inescapably, the IEP meeting itself. Given the IEP's status as a legal document that describes the special education and related services to be provided by the district to the student, the IEP meeting can be, and too often is, as much a time of conflict as it is a time of cooperation and partnership. It is naive to assume that all IEP meetings will be free of such tensions; even under the best circumstances, such important issues as placement or evaluation–eligibility decisions are difficult and can make for a tense meeting. It is all the more important that transition planning not contribute to conflict, but instead be a source of collaboration that can sustain the family–professional partnership. The first steps to ensuring that this is the case have already been discussed: forming alliances with families as advocates, listening to

TABLE 4.2
The Big Picture Transition Planning Analysis

Step	Activity to Do with Parent
Step 1: Present Picture	
History	List/discuss important events in the life of the student.
	List/discuss student's strengths, challenges.
Preferences	List student's favorite things.
Friends/Relationships	List student's friends, relatives, and social/emotional supports.
Community Access	Identify places, events, and activities student uses in community.
Living Arrangements	Identify where student currently lives and significant people in that setting.
School or Work	Identify present school or work arrangements.
Resource Management	Identify current resources, who manages them, and how they are managed.
Transportation	List ways in which student gets around community.
Step 2: Future Picture	
Living Arrangements	Identify where student would like to and will likely live.
Resource Management	Identify how student will manage resources with what supports.
School or Work	Identify what student would like in school program and future work.
Transportation	Discuss how student's future transportation needs will differ.
Community Access	Identify community activities in which student wants to/should participate.
Friends and Relationships	Identify ongoing and new relationships to foster or support.
Needs	List/discuss needs and supports to fulfill "big picture."
Self-Advocacy	Identify how to support enhanced choice and control.
Step 3: Big Picture Planning	
Priorities	Identify areas of high priority for student.
Solutions	Identify solutions for overcoming barriers and achieving prioritized goals.
Resources	List/discuss resources for overcoming barriers and achieving prioritized goals.
Most Promising Solutions	Identify most promising solutions and rank according to likely success.
Step 4: Action Plan	
Solutions	List prioritized solutions in sequential order.
Resources	Specify resources for priority areas.
Action	Develop action plan to achieve priority and take action.
Evaluation	Evaluate progress and revise as necessary.

Note. From *School and Community Integration Curriculum,* by J. McDonnell, 1992, Salt Lake City: University of Utah. Copyright 1992 by University of Utah. Reprinted with permission.

families and inviting their participation, forming family support groups and providing learning opportunities, and involving families in the information exchange process. If the only point of contact between the teacher and the family is an annual IEP meeting, then the family–school relationship is very unlikely to be collaborative, and may in fact be antagonistic.

Setting the Tone

One mandated objective of the IEP meeting is that the student's educational goals be determined by the IEP team, including transition-related goals. Schools vary in their treatment of the IEP meeting. Some schools regard it as an *information and instruction meeting,* in which one group (e.g., school personnel) gives information (e.g., about the educational program) to another group (parents, students). Such meetings are built on the "educator as expert" model, in which the meeting leader knows something that the other team members do not. Other schools regard it as a *consultation meeting,* in which the opinions or advice of various parties (parent, student, agency, or provider) are solicited and then incorporated into the final decision or program. The problem with a consultation model is that the one who sets up the meeting, in this case the school, is still in charge of decisions; the opinions or advice that are gathered in such a meeting can be heeded or discarded. Still other schools view IEP meetings as *team building meetings,* where stakeholders are brought together to get the team excited about the new program, which, by and large, has been determined prior to the meeting (Bormann & Bormann, 1972).

Despite the prevalence of these interpretations of IEP meetings, the IEP meeting is and must remain a collaborative *decision-making meeting.* Certainly aspects of consultation, information, or team building become part of the meeting, but the primary purpose of the meeting is to come to a decision about an educational program. The parent's or other family member's role is not simply as a recipient or provider of information, but as an active decision maker. Being an active decision maker means going through certain steps: (1) identifying the options available; (2) identifying the consequences of implementing each option, that is, examining the risks and benefits associated with that implementation; (3) weighing these benefits and risks with individual preferences and priorities; and (4) selecting a particular option. As discussed previously, many schools unnecessarily constrain the number of options available based on what programs are currently available or fail to take family preferences and priorities into account when weighing the risks and benefits of a decision. Active family involvement means meaningful participation in decision making.

Turnbull and Turnbull (1997) outline a model for IEP meetings that promotes active family decision making. They have identified eight components necessary for a collaborative IEP conference: (a) preparing in advance; (b) connecting and getting started; (c) sharing visions and great expectations; (d) reviewing formal evaluation and current levels of performance; (e) sharing resources, priorities, and concerns; (f) developing goals and objectives; (g) specifying placement and related services; and (h) summarizing and concluding. While some of the eight components have always been a part of traditional IEP meetings (e.g., reviewing formal evaluations, developing goals and objectives), several of the steps provide for opportunities for true collaboration (e.g., connecting and getting started; sharing visions and great expectations; sharing resources, priorities, and concerns). Using this model of IEP conferences, the student and family members are empowered to be active participants in the planning process.

Student and family involvement at IEP meetings is a critical first step toward ensuring effective transition planning. In fact, taking control of one's learning might be the most important aspect of transition. Students and families often talk about how transition continues long after school services end. In addition many students and families will continue to be involved in individualized planning meetings as a part of the adult service system. Therefore it makes sense that schools develop processes by which families and young adults with disabilities can develop the skills necessary to participate actively as equally contributing members at their IEP (and future individualized planning) meetings.

A final note on setting the tone of the IEP meeting: Be aware that the use of educational jargon and labels referring to students can derail the most sincere efforts to form a partnership. Professionals should minimize the use of jargon and acronyms and, when the use is absolutely necessary, should be sure that family members know what the jargon means before the meeting begins. Simply explaining what a particular acronym means emphasizes to many parents that they are outsiders in the process. The use of outdated labels (educable, trainable) can anger students and families and create an insurmountable gulf between school and home.

Deciding on Goals and Coming Prepared

Perhaps one of the most common, and fundamentally egregious, distortions of true family involvement in decision making is the practice of determining student goals and objectives prior to the meeting. The authors have personally witnessed numerous IEP meetings in which teachers, speech and occupational therapists, vocational coordinators, and other school personnel come to the IEP meeting with fully formed and completed IEP goals. In such circumstances, parents are told what the student will work on in class or therapy and are expected to sign on the dotted line with their approval. Subscribing to the myth that teachers and school personnel are "the experts" who know best, many parents willingly acquiesce to this plan. Practitioners often seem almost surprised when a few family members balk at this rubber-stamp process. Yet this factory-line method of establishing IEP goals has the dual impact of limiting family involvement and input as well as student involvement and is particularly problematic when the instructional area is transition.

Of course, teachers should still come to meetings prepared with potential goals and objectives to present to the team for consideration. In fact, if the transition planning process is viewed as an ongoing process, parents, other family members, and students will have contributed to the assessment process, exchanged information about instructional needs resulting from that assessment, discussed priorities for instruction both in and out of school, and may have drafted potential goals and objectives well in advance of the meeting. This is vastly different, however, from the traditional model of teacher-directed assessment, evaluation, and goal development. The IEP meeting should be a time during which previous discussions about transition-related goals are finalized, and new or different goals are generated based on student and family input. One way to empower families to take a more active role in the goal-setting process is to ask them to bring educational goals they want to see addressed to the meeting. Such goals could be put on the table along with student-identified goals (discussed in greater detail subsequently) and teacher or professional goals, and become among the options considered for adoption.

One such model developed by Furney and her colleagues (no date given on document) uses a modified MAPS process for transition planning. This MAPS process involves organizing one or two meetings prior to the transition IEP meeting. First, a modified MAPS meeting is held and the MAPS team completes the following steps and answers the questions specifically for information related to transition:

> Step 1: *History*—What is the student's history? This information is intended to be a snapshot of the student's life including topics such as schools attended, family life, friends, favorite places, etc.

Step 2: *Dreams*—What are the student's dreams for the future? This information encourages everyone to dream about the future and can be used later in the IEP process to develop goals for the student.

Step 3: *Fears*—What are the student's fears about the future? This step asks the group to talk about their fears, especially those that may be barriers to fulfilling the dreams. These fears may be both concrete or more general in nature.

Step 4: *Personal Qualities*—Who is the student? This is an opportunity for the group to focus on the student's strengths and contributions. The facilitator encourages members to talk about strengths, skills, likes, dislikes, personal qualities, favorite activities, etc.

Step 5: *Needs*—What are the needs now and after high school? This question allows the group to prioritize information for the IEP by brainstorming a list of issues and needs of the student as they specifically relate to achieving their desired future.

The next step in the process is either to schedule a second meeting or move to the next phase of the process. This next phase involves compiling all of the information gathered during the MAPS meeting, along with other relevant information, into a chart divided into four outcome areas: employment, independent living, postsecondary education, and community participation. As the team reviews the student's MAPS in relation to these four transition outcome areas, they identify potential goals and activities for the IEP. They can then transfer this information into the actual IEP. This phase could also be completed as a part of the actual IEP meeting, or the teacher or facilitator of the MAPS meeting could meet with the family and student to complete this phase prior to the IEP with feedback and input from the IEP team members at the actual meeting.

Allowing Students To Lead the Meeting

The traditional IEP meeting typically has a school professional designated as the chairperson or as the person completing the district paperwork. But older students, particularly those in the transition phase, can take an active role in their meetings, including, though not limited to, leading the meeting (Wehmeyer, Martin, & Sands, 1998; Wehmeyer & Sands, 1998). Promoting student involvement in transition, just like promoting family involvement, means that professionals must give up some power and authority and shift from the roles of expert and decision maker to the roles of collaborator and supporter.

Countryman and Schroeder (1996) examined the perceptions of and satisfaction with student-led conferences by parents and family members. Seventy-five percent of the parents involved indicated they preferred the student-led conferences over teacher-led conferences. The student-led conferences provided family members with a better understanding of the student's capacities and interests, and several parents felt that they received a more honest report of their child's performance. Countryman and Schroeder quote one parent as saying: "'Students seem more open and honest about their performance. I didn't get the sugar-coated reports from advisors, who tend to present negative aspects in a positive manner'" (p. 68).

This parent's perception of the process is, in essence, an indictment of the deficits-approach taken by some educators. Transition services need to accentuate the positive and focus on the students abilities, not just limitations. Lipsky and Gartner (1989) pointed out that if colleges were run like secondary special education programs, freshmen would identify what they do worst and spend four years improving slightly in that area. Professionals need to approach the transition process just as they do postsecondary education: by identifying what students do well and what they like and want, and then working to capitalize on these traits to enable students to achieve desired goals and outcomes.

When focusing on enhancing student involvement at the meeting, educators should be aware that parents will have some concerns. For example, Countryman and Schroeder (1996) noted that some parents were worried about the reduced participation of the professional in the meeting and felt that the student-led format discouraged them from discussing specific problems with the teacher. Again, the IEP meeting should not be the only time in which key stakeholders meet, and just as teachers and students should sometimes meet and talk separately, so too should teachers meet alone with parents to discuss their unique concerns and issues.

Another caveat to student-led meetings is that students need to learn that the IEP meeting is for collaborative decision making, and that their family members have a legitimate right to participate in decisions at the meeting. Research by Morningstar and colleagues (1995) discussed previously suggests that most students readily acknowledge this. Efforts to promote student involvement should not place sole emphasis on the student but on the student as one of the several key decision makers.

Finally, educators need to be aware of any cultural issues that might impinge upon the family's support for student-led meetings. The concepts of student-led IEPs and self-determination are based upon primarily Euro-American values that may conflict with other cultural groups (Turnbull & Turnbull, 1997). Therefore, educators must identify the values that each family and student place on issues such as independence and autonomy and work to resolve any conflicts.

To conclude, the need to build effective school–home partnerships is even more critical when a student has a significant disability. The student may need a variety of supports, and the family is likely to be the primary provider of these supports. Educators must therefore listen to the family and invite their participation in transition-related activities. Planning for the postschool period should begin early, not at the IEP meeting. A plan carefully refined over a number of years is more likely to be implemented with success, than one quickly devised at a single meeting.

CHAPTER 5

Parent Involvement in Transition Program Implementation

In a brochure, the Virginia Part H Assistance and Evaluation Project defined partnership as "a working relationship in which everyone's role is important and that which is done together is greater than what any one individual/group can do separately." This definition is especially true for the implementation of transition services, which can involve large numbers and varieties of participants. During transition the family and educators are like the two parts of a clasp. By cooperating with one another, they form the link between the much larger domains of community and school. The family must become involved in education by supporting the student's schoolwork at home and being active in school programs, including transition planning. The teacher must introduce aspects of community living, such as career options, into the education program, particularly during transition. This chapter looks at some of the specific responsibilities of both sides and the characteristics of the effective partnership they can create.

FAMILY RESPONSIBILITIES

Parents should be dreamers.

When a child is born, the parents have dreams that they hope the child will someday fulfill. Just because a child is given the label of a disability does not mean that parents should stop dreaming. The dreams may need to change somewhat, but it is crucial that parents keep dreaming and hoping. Frankly, if parents don't have dreams for their child, it is probable that no one else will have those dreams either. Holding low expectations for children with disabilities will guarantee that they will never achieve their potential.

Families should expect to talk a lot.

When families are part of the discussions about a child, they feel they are an integral piece of the process. As was discussed extensively in chapter 4, too many schools approach educational planning in a way that excludes meaningful participation on the part of the parents or family members. The same remains true in the implementation process. Family members need to remain active, equal participants, and teachers and professionals must continue to listen to ongoing family issues, concerns, and questions. Communication doesn't end at the close of the IEP meeting but should be a year-round dialogue.

Families should ask school personnel to be specific about what is needed.

The term "parent involvement" is heard everywhere, but the meaning seems to change depending on who is wanting this involvement. Families are not always sure what is expected of them, so they should ask for specific information. Once they know the details, they can tell the school personnel if some expectation cannot be fulfilled. Not all family members can be involved in the same way and to the same degree. For instance, some may be very comfortable completing all the paperwork associated with applying for various government programs, while others may be unable to perform this activity well.

Families should support the student's self-determination/ self-advocacy efforts.

Families must continue to encourage the student's efforts towards self-determination and self-advocacy. They can create a supportive environment in which the student can test abilities and limitations. They can help their child develop positive work habits and behaviors, self-determination skills, and the self-confidence to succeed. Davis and Wehmeyer (1991) suggested the following ten steps for families to promote independence and self-determination:

1. Walk the tightrope between protection and independence. Allow the child to explore.

2. Show that what the child says or does is important and can influence others.

3. Model your own sense of positive self-esteem for your child. Self-worth and self-confidence are critical factors in the development of self-determination.

4. Don't run away from questions from your child about differences related to her disability. On the other hand, don't focus unnecessarily on the negative side of the condition. Stress that everyone is individual, encourage your child's unique abilities, and help her accept unavoidable limitations.

5. Recognize the process of reaching goals; don't just emphasize outcomes.

6. Schedule opportunities for interactions with children of different ages and backgrounds.

7. Set realistic but ambitious expectations.

8. Allow your child to take responsibility for his own actions, both successes and failures.

9. Don't leave choice-making opportunities to chance.

10. Provide honest, positive feedback. Focus on the behavior or task that needs to be changed.

Families should keep the focus on present levels of performance and strengths instead of deficits.

No one likes to hear over and over again what he doesn't do well. Families have the responsibility to think about the child's strengths and how the transition program can build on those strengths to support a job and leisure activities.

Families should support the school's efforts to provide career development and job training.

An important part of an adult's life is holding a job. The family home is where the student learns about work-related demands, such as the importance of being dependable, on time, appropriately dressed, and so forth. If the family's culture and values are not compatible with what the school is suggesting with regard to jobs, then both the family and school must work to achieve a mutually agreeable solution.

Extended family and friends are good sources of information about the student's neighborhood and community. They can find out who are the contact people at different job sites and what businesses may be open to hiring a student with a disability. They can and should introduce teachers and job coaches to business connections, particularly to the individuals involved in hiring employees. Families should use their networks to help find work sites for career awareness, exploration, and training experiences.

A growing body of research indicates that family involvement may be a critical factor in postschool success (Halpern, Doren, & Benz, 1993; Heal & Rusch, 1995). For example, Heal and Rusch (1995) found that a student's personal characteristics (e.g., gender, ethnicity, living skills, academic skills) and family influences were the strongest predictors of employment, even more so than the student's vocational training opportunities (except for on-the-job training). The importance of the family's role was additionally confirmed by a recent series of focus groups consisting of students with a range of disabilities (Morningstar, 1997). These students asserted that their families were instrumental in influencing their career and job choices. The students also said they expected their families' ongoing support in helping them find jobs. That families influence career development for students without disabilities is not new (Hoffman, Hafacker, & Goldsmith, 1992; Super, 1990; Trice & Tillapaugh, 1991). In fact, the role that families play in career development has been established for all age levels including preschool (Vondracek & Kirchner, 1974), elementary school (Trice, 1991; Trice & McClellan, 1993), secondary school (McDonald & Jessell, 1992), and college (Hoffman et al., 1992).

Parents and extended family members typically help students to shape their career aspirations in informal and indirect ways, but particularly by serving as role models (Morningstar, 1997). In fact, as role models they provide a strong foundation for career development from the child's early years. This early influence demonstrates the importance of a lifespan approach to career development and transition (Hershenson & Szymanski, 1992; Szymanski, 1994).

TEACHER RESPONSIBILITIES

Teachers should ask families how they want to be involved.

Teachers need to determine ways that families feel comfortable and capable of contributing. They should create planning environments that acknowledge and encourage this involvement (Brotherson, Berdine, & Sartini, 1993). In addition, they must be aware of the importance of encouraging family participation without jeopardizing the personal choices and dignity of the student (Callahan & Garner, 1997) and without straining the family structure. They should keep in mind the family systems approach and not expect all families to provide explicit home learning experiences for their children with disabilities (Morningstar, 1997).

Teachers should create comprehensive career development programs.

Teachers should prepare programs that show families a variety of ways to help their children explore careers. Such programs could also inform educators about possible career interests and aspirations (Izzo, 1987). Programs should provide information in a variety of formats.

Teachers should view extended family members as possible role models.

Teachers should recognize that students' uncles, aunts, cousins, and grandparents can be as important as parents in providing positive career role models. In communities with high unemployment and other economic disadvantages, these extended family members are especially important because they expand the potential number of role models (Morningstar, 1997).

Teachers should keep in mind the lifespan approach to transition.

Teachers should encourage early expectations for families and students. Even parents of young children can begin to develop future career and lifestyle visions. Teachers can show examples of successful adults with disabilities in meaningful and valued careers (Brotherson et al., 1993).

Teachers should help families and students to "connect" with appropriate adult service personnel.

Many students and families report that they don't remember meeting transition and adult agency staff who may have attended one or two IEP meetings (Hanley-Maxwell et al., 1998; Morningstar, 1995). Families and students should have the opportunity to develop long-term relationships with these professionals.

Teachers should consider the additional supports that the family may be able to provide.

In order for the student to be employed, the family may need to provide support for getting ready in the morning, transportation, etc. Teachers should be aware that family members may "volunteer" to provide this support out of a sense of duty or because they feel pressure from the school. Teachers need to assess whether the family can really provide this consistent support over the long haul, or if conflicting responsibilities may arise (Callahan & Garner, 1997).

THE SUCCESSFUL PARTNERSHIP

The National PTA has set six "standards" for family involvement in schools, which are listed in Table 5.1 (PTA, no date). The quality indicators of these standards are as applicable to transition programs as they are to other educational programs, and are discussed here to provide direction for building successful partnerships.

Standard 1: Communication between home and school is regular, two-way, and meaningful.

As is emphasized throughout this monograph and in the PTA Standards, communication is the key to successful partnerships. The quality indicators of successful communication between home and school identified by the PTA include the use of a variety of communication tools on an ongoing basis; the establishment of opportunities for parents and educators to share information about the student; the dissemination of all school policies, processes, assessment activities, and school goals; and the scheduling of informal activities where parents and educators can interact. Translating communications for non-English speaking parents is critical.

TABLE 5.1
National Standards for Parent and Family Involvement Programs

Standard 1:	Communication between home and school is regular, two-way, and meaningful.
Standard 2:	Parenting skills are promoted and supported.
Standard 3:	Parents play an integral role in assisting student learning.
Standard 4:	Parents are welcome in the school, and their support and assistance are sought.
Standard 5:	Parents are full partners in the decisions that affect children and families.
Standard 6:	Community resources are used to strengthen schools, families, and student learning.

Note. From *National Standards for Parent/Family Involvement Programs,* written and published by Parent Teacher Association, n.d., Washington, DC.

Multiple communication tools should include mail, telephone, fax, e-mail, and other sources, as well as meetings for face-to-face communication. Teachers can create class newsletters; print family "handbooks" that contain all policies, processes, and school goals; and organize social events such as class picnics at times when families can reasonably attend. These social events promote communication between teacher and family as well as provide opportunities for families to become acquainted with one another. Educators can also write short descriptions about future activities involving the student and send these home to parents. The parents then know what to expect in each situation and can practice appropriate responses, if necessary. Finally, teachers can ask parents to brainstorm how they feel the student's strengths could be reinforced and expanded in each job or leisure setting. This allows the parents to feel a part of team and gives teachers new ideas.

Standard 2: Parenting skills are promoted and supported.

Children learn across multiple environments, and the home is every bit as much a "classroom" as is school. However, when teachers expect parents and family members to recreate the classroom in their home, they may create unfair stresses on the home environment. Families have unique roles in a child's development, and whatever time that the members spend with children is valuable. Effective school–home partnerships also help to link families to programs and resources within the community.

Standard 3: Parents play an integral role in assisting student learning.

Parental and student involvement in student learning are particularly important during transition, when family members take on roles of supporter, case manager, and even educator!

Standard 4: Parents are welcome in the school and their support and assistance are sought.

Schools need to create a climate in which parents, and parental input, is welcome. The school building, signage, and procedures should reflect that openness. Creating reliable allies by using parent expertise and resources is beneficial to the school.

Families, with their various interests and talents, represent opportunities for community learning as well as support for teachers and in-school personnel. The PTA quality indicators include organizing a simple, accessible program for using parent volunteers (including volunteer training), ensuring that parents who can't volunteer in the school building are provided other ways to contribute (at home or work), and showing appreciation for parental participation.

Standard 5: Parents are full partners in the decisions that affect children and families.

Parents and family members of children with disabilities, unlike other parents, are required by IDEA to participate in decision making.

Standard 6: Community resources are used to strengthen schools, families, and student learning.

Community resources are critical to successful schools and particularly to successful transition programs. Parents and family members are the key to community resources, from employment sites to social networks. Many schools and transition programs emphasize school–business partnerships, but these too often don't include parents and family members in the loop. Using families to find job sites, raise funds for transition program needs, address problem areas (transportation, lack of community support), and recruit other community members as partners (senior citizens, civic organizations, etc.) strengthens both the school's capacity to serve students and the school–home partnership.

CONCLUSION

Why invest the time and effort to bring parents and family members on board as equal partners and reliable allies? One answer is that it is the law. The real answer, however, is that it is one of the most important things a teacher can do to enable students to make a successful transition from school to adulthood. The National PTA has conducted a thorough review of the research into parental involvement. What did they conclude?

- When parents are involved, students achieve more, regardless of any other variable (socioeconomic status, parents' educational level, etc.).

- The more extensive the parent involvement, the higher the student achievement.

- When parents are involved, students exhibit more positive attitudes and behaviors.

- Students whose parents are involved have higher graduation rates and greater enrollment rates in postsecondary education.

- Junior and senior high school students whose parents remain involved, make better transitions, maintain the quality of their work, and develop realistic plans for the future (Henderson & Berla, 1995).

Probably there is no other action teachers can take as powerful and educationally effective as creating successful alliances with families. It is as simple as that: Effective transition programs must have meaningful, active, and equal family involvement. For students with disabilities, it is an investment that ensures a future of opportunities.

References

Bailey, D. B., Jr., Buysse, V., Smith, T., & Elam, J. (1992). The effects and perceptions of family involvement in program decisions about family-centered practices. *Evaluation and Program Planning, 15,* 23–32.

Berry, J. O., & Hardman, M. (1998). *Lifespan perspectives on the family and disability.* Needham Heights, MA: Allyn and Bacon.

Blackorby, J., & Wagner, M. (1996). Longitudinal postschool outcomes for youth with disabilities: Findings from the National Longitudinal Transition Study. *Exceptional Children, 62*(5), 399–413.

Blue-Banning, M. J. (1997). *The transition of Hispanic adolescents with disabilities to adulthood: Parent and professional perspectives.* Unpublished dissertation, University of Kansas, Lawrence.

Bormann, E. G., & Bormann, N. C. (1972). *Effective small group communication.* Edina, MN: Burgess.

Brotherson, M. J., Backus, L. H., Summers, J. A., & Turnbull, A. P. (1986). Transition to adulthood. In J. A. Summers (Ed.), *The right to grow up: An introduction to adults with developmental disabilities* (pp. 17–44). Baltimore: Brookes.

Brotherson, M. J., Berdine, W. H., & Sartini, V. (1993). Transition to adult services: Support for ongoing parent participation. *Remedial and Special Education, 14*(4), 44–51.

Brotherson, M. J., Cook, C. C., Cunconan-Lahr, R., & Wehmeyer, M. L. (1995). Policy supporting self-determination in environments of children with disabilities. *Education and Training in Mental Retardation and Developmental Disabilities, 30*(1), 3–13.

Brotherson, M. J., Houghton, J., Turnbull, A. P., Bronicki, G. J., Roeder-Gordon, C., Summers, J. A., & Turnbull, H. R. (1988). Transition into adulthood: Parental planning for sons and daughters with disabilities. *Education and Training in Mental Retardation, 23*(3), 165–174.

Brotherson, M. J., & Spillers, C. S. (1989). *A qualitative study on families with disability at two periods of transition in the life cycle.* Unpublished manuscript. University of Kentucky, Lexington.

Callahan, M. J., & Garner, J. B. (1997). *Keys to the workplace: Skills and supports for people with disabilities.* Baltimore: Brookes.

Carter, E., & McGoldrick, M. (Eds.). (1980). *The family life cycle.* New York: Garden Press.

Clark, G. (1998). *Assessment for transitions planning.* Austin, TX: PRO-ED.

Clay, J. A. (1992). Native American independent living. *Rural and Special Education Quarterly, 11*(1), 41–51.

Countryman, L. L., & Schroeder, M. (1996). When students lead parent-teacher conferences. *Educational Leadership, 53*(7), 64–68.

Cutler, B. C. (1993). *You, your child, and special education: A guide to making the system work.* Baltimore: Brookes.

Davis, S., & Wehmeyer, M. L. (1991). *Promoting self-determination in the home.* Arlington, TX: The Arc of the United States.

Developmental Disabilities Assistance and Bill of Rights Act. (1990). Public Law 101-496.

Dunst, C. J., Johnson, C., Trivette, C. M., & Hamby, D. (1991). Family-oriented early intervention policies and practices: Family-centered or not? *Exceptional Children, 58*(2), 115–126.

Education of All Handicapped Children Act of 1975, 20 U.S.C. §1400 *et seq.*

Education of the Handicapped Act Amendments of 1983, 20 U.S.C. §1400 *et seq.*

Ferguson, P. M., & Ferguson, D. L. (1993). The promise of adulthood. In M. E. Snell (Ed.), *Instruction of students with severe disabilities* (4th ed., pp. 588–608). New York: Merrill.

Ferguson, P. M., Ferguson, D. L., & Jones, D. (1988). Generations of hope: Parental perspectives on the transition of their children with severe retardation from school to adult life. *Journal of the Association for Persons with Severe Disabilities, 13,* 177–187.

Field, S., & Hoffman, A. (1994). Development of a model for self-determination. *Career Development for Exceptional Individuals, 159*–169.

Flaxman, E., & Inger, M. (1991). Parents and schooling in the 1990s. *The ERIC Review, 1*(3), 2–6.

Furney, K. S. (no date). *Making dreams happen: How to facilitate the MAPS process.* Burlington: Vermont Systems Change Project.

Gallivan-Felon, A. (1994). "Their Senior Year": Family and service provider perspectives on the transition from school to adult life for young adults with disabilities. *Journal of the Association for Persons with Severe Disabilities, 19,* 11–23.

Gerber, P. J., Ginsberg, R., & Reiff, H. B. (1992). Identifying alterable patterns in employment success for high successful adults with learning disabilities. *Journal of Learning Disabilities, 25*(8), 475–487.

Halpern, A. (1985). Transition: A look at the foundations. *Exceptional Children, 57*(6), 479–486.

Halpern, A. (1993). Quality of life as a conceptual framework for evaluating transition outcomes. *Exceptional Children, 59,* 486–498.

Halpern, A., Doren, B., & Benz, M. (1993). Job experiences of students with disabilities during their last two years in school. *Career Development for Exceptional Individuals, 16*(1), 63–74.

Halpern, A., & Wehmeyer, M. L. (1998). *Transition: Where have we been and where are we going?* A manuscript submitted for publication.

Halvorsen, A. T., Doering, K., Farron-Davis, F., Usilton, R., & Sailor, W. (1989). The role of parents and family members in planning severely disabled students' transitions from school. In W. Sailor, J. L. Anderson, A. T. Halvorsen, K. Doering, J. Filler, & L. Goetz (Eds.), *The comprehensive local school: Regular education for all students with disabilities* (pp. 253–267). Baltimore: Brookes.

Hanley-Maxwell, C., Pogoloff, S. M., & Whitney-Thomas, J. (1998). Families: The heart of transition. In F. Rusch & J. Chadsey (Eds.), *Beyond high school: Transition from school to work* (pp. 234–264). Belmont, CA: Wadsworth.

Hanley-Maxwell, C., Whitney-Thomas, J., & Pogoloff, S. M. (1995). The second shock: Parental perspectives of their child's transition from school to adult life. *Journal of the Association for Persons with Severe Disabilities, 20,* 3–16.

Hanson, M. J., & Carta, J. J. (1996). Addressing the challenges of families with multiple risks. *Exceptional Children, 62*(3), 201–212.

Harry, B. (1992). *Cultural diversity, families, and the special education system.* New York: Teachers College Press.

Harry, B., Allen, N., & McLaughlin, M. (1995). Communication versus compliance: African-American parents' involvement in special education. *Exceptional Children, 61*(4), 364–377.

Harry, B., Grenot-Scheyer, M., Smith-Lewis, M., Park, H., Xin, F., & Schwartz, I. (1995). Developing culturally inclusive services for individuals with severe disabilities. *Journal of the Association for Persons with Severe Handicaps, 20*(2), 99–109.

Harry, B., & Kalyanpur, M. (1994). Cultural underpinnings of special education: Implications for professional interactions with culturally diverse families. *Disability & Society, 9*(2), 145–165.

Heal, L. W., & Rusch, F. R. (1995). Predicting employment for students who leave special education high school programs. *Exceptional Children, 61,* 472–487.

Henderson, A., & Berla, N. (1995). *A new generation of evidence: The family is critical to student achievement.* Washington, DC: National PTA.

Hernandez, D. J. (1994). Children's changing access to resources: A historical perspective. *Society for Research in Child Development Social Policy Report, 8*(1), 1–23.

Hershenson , D. B., & Szymanski, E. M. (1992). Career development of people with disabilities. In R. M. Parker & E. M. Szymanski (Eds.), *Rehabilitation counseling: Basics and beyond* (2nd ed., pp. 273–303). Austin, TX: PRO-ED.

Hoffman, J. J., Hafacker, C., & Goldsmith, E. B. (1992). How closeness affects parental influence on business college students' career choices. *Journal of Career Development, 19*(1), 65–73.

Hutchins, M. P., & Renzaglia, A. (1998). Interviewing families for effective transition to employment. *Teaching Exceptional Children, 30*(4), 72–78.

Individuals with Disabilities Education Act of 1990, 20 U.S.C. §1400 *et seq.*

Individuals with Disabilities Education Act Amendments of 1997, 20 U.S.C. §1400 *et seq.*

Irvin, L. K., Thorin, E., & Singer, G. H. S. (1993). Family-related roles and considerations: Transition to adulthood by youth with developmental disabilities. *Journal of Vocational Rehabilitation, 3,* 38–46.

Izzo, M. V. (1987). Career development of disabled youth: The parents' role. *Journal of Career Development, 13*(4), 47–55.

Kohler, P. D. (1993). Best practices in transition: Substantiated or implied? *Career Development for Exceptional Individuals, 16,* 107–121.

Lichtenstein, S. (1993). Transition from school to adulthood: Case studies of adults with learning disabilities who dropped out of school. *Exceptional Children, 59,* 336–347.

Lichtenstein., S. (1998). Characteristics of youth and young adults. In F. R. Rusch & J. G. Chadsey (Eds.), *Beyond high school: Transition from school to work.* Belmont, CA: Wadsworth.

Lipsky, D. K., & Gartner, A. (1989). The current situation. In D. K. Lipsky & A. Gartner (Eds.), *Beyond separate education: Quality education for all* (pp. 3–24). Baltimore: Brookes.

Lubetkin, M. T. (1996). How teamwork transformed a neighborhood. *Educational Leadership, 53*(7), 10–12.

Luera, M. (1994). *Understanding family uniqueness through cultural diversity.* Albuquerque, NM: Alta Mira Specialized Family Services.

Martin, J. E., & Marshall, L. H. (1996). ChoiceMaker: Infusing self-determination instruction into the IEP and transition process. In D. J. Sands & M. L. Wehmeyer (Eds.), *Self-determination across the life span: Independence and choice for people with disabilities* (pp. 215–236). Baltimore: Brookes.

Martin, J. R. (1992). *The Schoolhome: Rethinking schools for changing families.* Cambridge, MA: Harvard University Press.

McDonald, J. L., & Jessell, J. C. (1992). Influence of selected variables on occupational attitudes and perceived occupational abilities of young adolescents. *Journal of Career Development, 18*(4), 239–250.

McDonnell, J. (1992). *School and community integration curriculum.* Salt Lake City: University of Utah.

McDonnell, J., Mathot-Buckner, C., & Ferguson, B. (1996). *Transition programs for students with moderate/severe disabilities.* Pacific Grove, CA: Brooks/Cole.

McFadden, D. L., & Burke, E. P. (1991). Developmental disabilities and the new paradigm: Directions for the 1990s. *Mental Retardation, 29,* iii–vi.

McGoldrick, M., & Carter, E. A. (1982). The family life cycle. In F. Walsh (Ed.), *Normal family processes* (pp. 167–195). New York: The Guilford Press.

McNair, J., & Rusch, F. R. (1991). Parent involvement in transition programs. *Mental Retardation, 29,* 93–101.

Mederer, H., & Hill, R. (1983). Critical transition over the family life span: Theory and research. In H. I. McCubbin, M. B. Sussman, & J. M. Patterson (Eds.), *Social stress and the family: Advances and development in family stress theory and research* (pp. 39–60). New York: The Haworth Press.

Michaels, C. A. (1998). *Transition to employment.* Austin, TX: PRO-ED.

Morningstar, M. E. (1995). *Examining the transition planning process: What are perceptions of students with disabilities regarding their transition from school to adult life?* Unpublished dissertation, University of Kansas, Department of Special Education, Lawrence.

Morningstar, M. E. (1997). Critical issues in career development and employment preparation for adolescents with disabilities. *Remedial and Special Education, 18*(5), 307–320.

Morningstar, M. E., Lattin, D. L., & Steinle, D. G. (1995). *Transition policy implementation in Kansas: A report of statewide focus groups.* Lawrence: University of Kansas.

Morningstar, M. E., Turnbull, A. P., & Turnbull, H. R. (1995). What do students with disabilities tell us about the importance of family involvement in the transition from school to adult life? *Exceptional Children, 62,* 249–260.

Morningstar, M. E., Turnbull, H. R., Reichard, A., & Umbarger, G. (1998). *The transition from school to adult life for students supported by medical technology.* Unpublished manuscript, Beach Center on Families and Disability, University of Kansas.

Navarrete, L. A., & White, W. J. (1994). School to community transition planning: Factors to consider when working with culturally diverse students and families in rural settings. *Rural and Special Education Quarterly, 13*(1), 51–56.

Parent Teacher Association. (n.d.). *National standards for parent/family involvement programs.* Washington, DC: Author.

Powell, T. H., & Gallagher, P. A. (1993). *Brothers and sisters: A special part of exceptional families* (2nd ed.). Baltimore: Brookes.

Powers, L., Singer, G. H. S., & Sowers, J. (1996). *On the road to autonomy: Promoting self-competence in children and youth with disabilities.* Baltimore: Brookes.

Rehabilitation Act Reauthorization. (1992). Public Law 102-569.

Sailor, W. (1994). *Inclusive practices in community services for culturally diverse young adults with disabilities.* Unpublished grant application, University Affiliated Programs, University of Kansas, Lawrence.

Sailor, W., Anderson, J. L., Halvorsen, A. T., Doering, K., Filler, J., & Goetz, L. (1989). *The comprehensive local school: Regular education for all students with disabilities.* Baltimore: Brookes.

Sale, P., Metzler, H., Everson, J. M., & Moon, M. S. (1991). Quality indicators of successful vocational transition programs. *Journal of Vocational Rehabilitation, 1*(4), 47–63.

Sands, D. J., & Wehmeyer, M. L. (1996). *Self-determination across the life span: Independence and choice for people with disabilities.* Baltimore: Brookes.

Seltzer, M. M., Krauss, M. W., & Janicki, M. P. (Eds.). (1994). *Life course perspectives on adulthood and old age.* Washington, DC: American Association on Mental Retardation.

Shafer, M. S., & Rangasamy, R. (1995). Transition and Native American youth: A follow-up study of school leavers on the Fort Apache Indian reservation. *Journal of Rehabilitation, 61*(1), 60–65.

Shank, M. S., & Turnbull, A. P. (1993). Cooperative family problem-solving: An intervention for single-parent families of children with disabilities. In G. H. S. Singer & L. E. Powers (Eds.), *Families, disability, and empowerment: Active coping skills and strategies for family interventions.* Baltimore: Brookes.

Shelton, T. L., Jeppson, E. S., & Johnson, B. H. (1989). *Family-centered care for children with special health needs.* Washington, DC: ACCH.

Sinclair, M. F., & Christenson, S. L. (1992). Home-school collaboration: A building block of empowerment. *IMPACT Feature Issue on Family Empowerment, 5*(2), 12–13.

Singer, G. H. S., & Powers, L. E. (1993). Contributing to resilience in families: An overview. In G. H. S. Singer & L. E. Powers (Eds.), *Families, disability, and empowerment: Active coping skills and strategies for family interventions* (pp. 1–25). Baltimore: Brookes.

Sitlington, P. L., Frank, A. R., & Carson, R. (1991). *Iowa statewide follow-up study: Changes in the adult adjustment of graduates with mental disabilities one vs. three years out of school.* Des Moines: Iowa Department of Education.

Sitlington, P. L., Frank, A. R., & Cooper, L. (1989). *Iowa statewide follow-up study: Adult adjustment of individuals with learning disabilities one year after leaving school.* Des Moines: Iowa Department of Education.

Slovic, R. (1990, December). *The family transition planning and support system: How does it work and what are the outcomes?* Paper presented at the 17th Annual Convention of the Association for Persons with Severe Handicaps.

Sonnenschein, P. (1981). Parents and professionals: An uneasy relationship. *Teaching Exceptional Children, 14,* 62–65.

Spekman, N. J., Goldberg, R. J., & Herman, K. L. (1992). Learning disabled children grow up: A search for factors related to success in the young adult years. *Learning Disabilities Research & Practice, 7,* 161–170.

Stineman, R. M., Morningstar, M. E., Bishop, B., & Turnbull, H. R. (1993). Role of families in transition planning for young adults with disabilities: Toward a method of person-centered planning. *Journal of Vocational Rehabilitation, 3*(2), 52–61.

Summers, J. A., Dell-Oliver, C., Turnbull, A. P., Benson, H. A., Santelli, E., Campbell, M., & Siegel-Causey, E. (1990). Examining the individualized family service plan process: What are family and practitioner preferences? *Topics in Early Childhood Special Education, 10*(1), 78–99.

Super, D. E. (1990). A life-span, life-space approach to career development. In D. Brown, L. Brooks, & Associates (Eds.), *Career choice and development: Applying contemporary theories to practice* (2nd ed.). San Francisco: Jossey-Bass.

Szymanski, E. (1994). Transition: Life-span and life-space considerations for empowerment. *Exceptional Children, 60,* 402–410.

Terkelson, K. G. (1980). Toward a theory of the family life cycle. In E. Carter & M. McGoldrick (Eds.), *The family life cycle.* New York: Garden Press.

Trice, A. D. (1991). A retrospective study of career development: I. Relationship among first aspirations, parental occupations, and current occupations. *Psychological Reports, 68,* 287–290.

Trice, A. D., & McClellan, N. (1993). Do children's career aspirations predict adult occupations? An answer from a secondary analysis of a longitudinal study. *Psychological Reports, 72,* 368–370.

Trice, A. D., & Tillapaugh, P. (1991). Children's estimates of their parents' job satisfaction. *Psychological Reports, 69,* 62–66.

Turbiville, V. P., Turnbull, A. P., Garland, C. W., & Lee, I. M. (1996). Development and implementation of IFSPs and IEPs: Opportunities for empowerment. In S. Odom & M. McLean (Eds.), *Early intervention /early childhood special education: Recommended practices* (pp. 77–100). Austin, TX: PRO-ED.

Turnbull, A. P., Barber, P., Behr, S., & Kerns, G. M. (1988). The family of children and youth with exceptionalities: A systems perspective. In E. Meyen & T. Skrtic (Eds.), *Exceptional children and youth: Traditional and emerging perspectives.* (3rd. ed.). Denver, CO: Love.

Turnbull, A. P., Blue-Banning, M. J., Anderson, E. L., Turnbull, H. R., Seaton, K. A., & Dinas, P. A. (1996). Enhancing self-determination through group action planning: A holistic emphasis. In D. J. Sands & M. L. Wehmeyer (Eds.), *Self-determination across the life span: Independence and choice for people with disabilities* (pp. 237–256). Baltimore: Brookes.

Turnbull, A. P., & Morningstar, M. E. (1993). Family and professional interaction. In M. Snell (Ed.), *Instruction of students with severe disabilities* (4th ed.). New York: Merrill.

Turnbull, A. P., Summers, J. A., & Brotherson, M. J. (1984). Family life cycle: Theoretical and empirical implications and future directions for families with mentally retarded members. In J. J. Gallagher & D. M. Vietze (Eds.), *Families of handicapped persons: Research, programs, and policy issues* (pp. 25–44). Baltimore: Brookes.

Turnbull, A. P., & Turnbull, H. R. (1978). *Parents speak out: Views from the other side of the two-way mirror.* Columbus, OH: Merrill.

Turnbull, A. P., & Turnbull, H. R. (1990). *Families, professionals, and exceptionality: A special partnership* (2nd ed.). Columbus, OH: Merrill.

Turnbull, A. P., & Turnbull, H. R. (1996). Self-determination within a culturally responsive family systems perspective: Balancing the family mobile. In L. E., Powers, G. H. S. Singer, & J. A. Sowers (Eds.), *On the road to autonomy: Promoting self-competence in children and youth with disabilities* (pp. 195–220). Baltimore: Brookes.

Turnbull, A. P., & Turnbull, H. R. (1997). *Families, professionals, and exceptionality: A special partnership* (3rd ed.). Upper Saddle River, NJ: Merrill/Prentice Hall.

Turnbull A. P., Turnbull, H. R., & Blue-Banning, M. J. (1994). Enhancing inclusion of infants and toddlers with disabilities and their families: A theoretical and programmatic analysis. *Infants and Young Children, 7*(2), 1–14.

Van Reusen, A. K., Bos, C. S., Schumaker, J. B., & Deshler, D. D. (1994). *The self-advocacy strategy for education and transition planning.* Lawrence, KS: Edge Enterprises, Inc.

Vondracek, S. I., & Kirchner, E. P. (1974). Vocational development in early childhood: An examination of young children's expressions of vocational aspirations. *Journal of Vocational Behavior, 5,* 251–260.

Ward, M. J., & Halloran, W. D. (1993, Fall). Transition issues for the 1990s. *OSERS News in Print: Transitions, 6*(1), 4–5.

Wehmeyer, M. L. (1998). Self-determination and individuals with significant disabilities: Examining meanings and misinterpretations. *Journal of the Association for Persons with Severe Handicaps, 23,* 5–16.

Wehmeyer, M. L., Agran, M., & Hughes, C. (1998). *Teaching self-determination to students with disabilities: Basic skills for successful transition.* Baltimore: Brookes.